BECOMING
MySelf

A Soul Journey with
Chronic Illness and Disability

Darrell Lynn Jones

BALBOA.
PRESS

A DIVISION OF HAY HOUSE

Cover illustration by Jon Marken
Photo of Darrell Lynn Jones by Dawn Heinsohn

Balboa Press books may be ordered through booksellers or by contacting:

Balboa Press
A Division of Hay House
1663 Liberty Drive
Bloomington, IN 47403
www.balboapress.com
1 (877) 407-4847

Because of the dynamic nature of the Internet, any web addresses or links contained in this book may have changed since publication and may no longer be valid. The views expressed in this work are solely those of the author and do not necessarily reflect the views of the publisher, and the publisher hereby disclaims any responsibility for them.

The author of this book does not dispense medical advice or prescribe the use of any technique as a form of treatment for physical, emotional, or medical problems without the advice of a physician, either directly or indirectly. The intent of the author is only to offer information of a general nature to help you in your quest for emotional and spiritual well-being. In the event you use any of the information in this book for yourself, which is your constitutional right, the author and the publisher assume no responsibility for your actions.

Any people depicted in stock imagery provided by Thinkstock are models, and such images are being used for illustrative purposes only. Certain stock imagery © Thinkstock.

Print information available on the last page.

ISBN: 978-1-5043-4056-4 (sc)
ISBN: 978-1-5043-4057-1 (hc)
ISBN: 978-1-5043-4055-7 (e)

Library of Congress Control Number: 2015914557

Balboa Press rev. date: 09/24/2015

To the thousands of individuals with disabilities and chronic illnesses who have passed through my life over four decades: your light came shining through and touched me in ways I can never describe.

Contents

Acknowledgments

The actual writing of this book took about seventeen months to complete. I started keeping notes in a journal more than ten years ago, and I thought they had the potential to be part of a book someday. But it was not until I joined Jenna Avery's online Writer's Circle in December of 2013 that I started to believe I could actually complete a manuscript. I want to thank my circle mates and the circle's coach, Terri Fedonczak. I may have been able to finish this manuscript on my own, but I doubt the process would have been as easy and fun as it was with their liberal encouragement and reinforcement.

I am deeply grateful to Janine Bertram Kemp for her helpful editorial feedback, bringing clarity and polish to parts of the manuscript that my tired writer's eyes could no longer see.

As many authors have stated, there really isn't enough room to acknowledge all the people whose presence in and around my life has added to the fascinating journey I have been privileged to experience. There have been a number of people, however, who have contributed so significantly to the journey I write about, that I want to acknowledge them here.

I want to say thank you to the late Joseph Parella Jr. and Patricia Laird for opening the door to the world of disability rights for me. Thank you to George Ebert, Patricia Miller, the late Richard Miller, Marilyn Saviola, and the "homeless" man who lives in the park—whose name I do not know—for educating me about the real meaning of self-determination.

Thank you to Anne-Marie Hughey for believing in me and giving me a chance to try employment again when I was worn and weary from trying to prove that I was sick.

Thank you to Richard Petty and Lex Frieden for continuing that belief and giving me the opportunity to hit my creative stride. My love and gratitude go to Sharon Finney, Marjorie Elhardt, Carol Eubanks, Dawn Heinsohn, and Paula McElwee for being a joyous circle of support every day in the adventure we call the independent living movement.

Thank you to Michael Crinnin, Burt Danovitz, Bruce Darling, the late Pat Figueroa, Denise Figueroa, Tim Fuchs, and Bob Michaels for being my teachers in so many ways.

Dr. Judith Holt's kind mentoring always lifts me up to be all that I can be, and I am blessed to have her in my life.

Thank you to the Meeks clan, my caring cousins and their families who surround me with acceptance and generosity.

Thank you to my friends and supporters Gillian Bower, Lorraine Kreimeyer, Cathy Kurvers, and Carri Lynn George who have been there for me emotionally through the ups and downs of my life for many years. They never forgot who I am—even when I did.

I want to acknowledge my former husband, Norman Leslie Jones Jr., for playing a leading role in the process of becoming myself and my talented artist-writer-world-traveling sister, Frances Carter, for modeling how to follow a dream.

Thank you to Mary Lamielle, Susan Molloy, and Amina Kruck for helping me find my own voice as a person with an invisible chronic illness within the disability rights and independent living movements.

And last, but not least, my profound gratitude goes to Ava Brenner and The Guys and Shaina Noll for holding a flashlight while I find my way in the dark.

Preface

Throughout this book, I use the term *mechanical* to explain certain things that brought about a change in my life. I'm using the word to mean some real action or event that contributed to the change. The fact that I began to notice that things were mechanical is the very reason those things made a difference in my life. I had been a great believer in magical thinking, creating the reality that I wanted, and good old-fashioned faith, but I had believed in those things as woo-woo phenomena that had no substance. When none of those things cured me of multiple chemical sensitivity, fibromyalgia, and chronic fatigue syndrome, I experienced a deep crisis of confidence in all the things I had believed about the way the universe works.

From that crisis, I began to find spiritual teachers in unexpected places who cleared up the mystery for me. It wasn't positive thinking that gave me the resources to live my life more effectively. It was real thinking instead that accomplished that. It was a concept that brought me in through the back door of my life so I could see it from a more grounded perspective. Once grounded, the relationship with my spiritual self began to make sense.

Another word I use a great deal is myself. Self is one of those electrically charged words in our world today. Although our understanding of that word has broadened in the past few decades through our exploration of such concepts as self-help programs, self-determination, self-esteem, self-respect, self-worth, selfishness, selflessness, self-control, self-made, and greater self, some of us still get a bit squirrely when we're trying to sort out its place in the scheme of things.

We may not be sure how much we are allowed to love and nurture ourselves versus what is due to other people, things, and activities. Our rhetoric has changed on that count in recent years, but an inner struggle continues for many of us. Some of us are also not sure who we're talking about when we refer to our self. And more to the point for those of us with chronic illness, what does the self have to do with our physical or mental conditions?

The word *myself* can stir feelings of guilt, but this book is entirely about finding, then becoming myself—that whole, integrated, being who I am. In many places throughout the book, the word Self is capitalized. That is my way of denoting that I'm talking about our total being, which includes the greater self.

There are indications that there is growing desire all over the world to live more meaningful and conscious lives, letting go of what is unimportant and staying focused on what really matters to us. For many people with serious chronic illnesses, that can seem an elusive goal because so many of us have believed that being sick means there's something wrong with us. When we embrace the understanding that *who we are* is not wrong, finding meaning in our lives can involve some very different pathways of travel.

If you live with chemical sensitivities, fibromyalgia, chronic fatigue syndrome, or any chronic illness or disability for that matter—and feel defective, punished, or devalued because of it—it is my hope that this book will help you reframe the illness or disability. My good fortune to have amazing spiritual teachers and work in the disability rights arena has given me a rare insight into possibilities that I want to share.

Introduction

Your life is a series of opportunities to become yourself.
—Alan Cohen[1]

Those of us who live with chronic illnesses have unprecedented access to healing modalities and live in an age where pursuing *consciousness* and the meaning of life, including trying to understand the experience of chronic illness, are no longer questionable pursuits. We are in ample company if we want to find healing and purpose.

Physicians have a lower risk of losing their medical licenses if they practice integrative and holistic medicine. And what more real indicator could there be than to have a highly acclaimed television doctor such as Dr. Oz talking freely about herbs, yoga, and acupuncture to a huge following of eager students? Dr. Oz has his detractors, but they may discover it's very hard to stop an idea whose time has come. Popular spiritual thought leaders such as Oprah Winfrey, Wayne Dyer, Caroline Myss, Eckhart Tolle, and Ram Dass have opened doors to territories that many of us quietly explored for years, hoping it would someday become acceptable for us to explore them openly. And so it has.

Many of us who experience debated and disputed conditions such as fibromyalgia (FM), chronic fatigue syndrome (CFS), multiple chemical sensitivity (MCS, which is also known as environmental illness), and a number of other invisible chronic illnesses operated behind closed doors in both physical and spiritual realms for a long time because these illnesses were viewed with skepticism. Doctors, counselors, family members, friends, employers, and coworkers dismissed us. We were told our symptoms were imaginary, psychological, or exaggerated. Some people said they were a spiritual failing.

Illnesses such as MCS and Gulf War Syndrome became political wherein some of us have been involved in policy arguments about indoor air quality in public places or have attempted to access medical benefits and services that we believe we have a right to. In this process, some of us sensed that we had lost a part of ourselves because we felt rejected and invalidated as human beings. Some of us have dealt with two layers of realities: the body-wide pain, fatigue, neurological and cognitive dysfunction, chronic infections, food sensitivities, digestive problems, and a host of other physical and mental symptoms on the one hand and an apparent lack of useful support on the other.

These types of illnesses can be terrifying, maddening, and awful to live with. The systemic effect on nearly every bodily function can make us wonder if we will be able to get through the day. Some of us are confined to our homes or even our beds. Those of us who are well enough to get out and about may feel like we're negotiating a minefield, dodging chemicals, activities that deplete us, and comments that wound us.

Where specific recommendations for treatments and protocols have been forthcoming, we have found a mountain of information, but it is often conflicting, expensive, and not covered by insurance. It can be confusing, especially when viewed through a brain-fogged mind. When suggested treatments have been covered by insurance, we may have found that we couldn't tolerate the prescribed medication or that the cure was worse than the disease.

Where treatments have not been recommended, we have often been on the receiving end of comments about the psychological nature of the conditions. Doctors may have said, "You just need to relax," "Have you considered counseling?" or "All your tests were negative." That one usually ends the discussion.

People we love may have said, "You really could get up out of that bed if you wanted to—mind over matter, you know" or "You're just trying to get out of [fill in the blank]." Our relationships may have been tangled up with guilt on our part or theirs—or both. We may have been told we don't really want to get well if we're not willing to go bankrupt paying for every treatment that's recommended. Some of us have gone bankrupt because we had to stop working; a third layer of financial hardship and a fourth layer of shame may have been added to our experiences.

Those of us who turned to an exploration of spirituality in search of meaning and healing may have found another place of confusion instead. For a long time, my own measure of spiritual growth was whether or not implementing the principles I was learning healed my physical condition. It was a quest with an expected prize. After the race, I could hold it up, providing proof to the world that I was an acceptable human being.

Some of us believed that traditional religious faith would result in a cure. We thought that if we worshiped and praised God, prayed, read scripture, and believed, believed, believed, our faithfulness would restore our health. Oh, how I contemplated that grain of mustard seed.

Numerous friends and strangers have said, "We have a faith healer coming to our church next Sunday. Why don't you come and be healed?" How could they know I had already tried that numerous times?

We may have grown up believing the childlike notion that if we wished upon a star with all our might, our every desire would come true.

Concepts of creating your own reality and the law of attraction led many of us to think that health and wellness were just around the corner. Thinking positive thoughts, saying affirmations, choosing happiness, meditating, staying in the present moment, becoming conscious of who we really are (we're not our illnesses), and setting our intentions for what we want are practices that are now readily accessible to average citizens. Many of us realized that such ideas are not in conflict with our preferred religions; in fact, they were inherent to our religions all along.

We may have been introduced to terms such as *mysticism, bioenergetics, energy healing, psychoneuroimmunology, consciousness and beingness, quantum physics, archetypes, mindfulness, and mind-body-spirit holism.* Even if we leaned toward more traditional, Western medical approaches, we've probably at least been exposed to these ideas. There is an expanded view on the planet of what's possible in the realm of altering reality.

There are a number of people who experienced FM, CFS, MCS, and other chronic illnesses who have reported that they have been cured through specific medical protocols, alternative healing modalities, or faith healing. I believe those stories. I have never doubted that such things were possible in spite of the fact that I continue to be sick. It was the process of sorting out why wellness resulted for some people and not (yet) for me that is my story. The story is still unfolding, and I spend my days focusing on being present with what is before me now rather than believing that a cure is the only acceptable outcome.

It would be a bonus for me if anything I share here is useful for someone else, but I'm primarily writing this manuscript for myself. I want to be heard. Even if no one else ever reads what I've written, I am finally hearing myself in a way that I've never experienced with any other opportunity. It is not only the illness that seems invisible to the world; I felt for a long time that my very presence on the planet was invisible. Being able to see words on a computer monitor that I have written about my experience is one of the most effective healing therapies I have utilized. It has caused me to dig deep into my beliefs and feelings. Writing as medicine is not overrated.

The other piece of motivation is that what I've experienced has been so profound and transformative, I want to express it. Whether or not it has any value or meaning to anyone else, it has value to me. It is a record of something precious.

Even so, if there is something here that you can use, I am delighted. One day, I was so angry with all the doctors and teachers I had listened to, I found myself yelling into the ethers, "Will somebody please just tell me how to get through the next ten minutes!"

When I was at my sickest, books about living with these conditions helped me survive. Nearly thirty years later, I still have deep gratitude for Elizabeth Rose's *Lady of Gray Healing Candida: The Nightmare Chemical Epidemic*. I have vivid memories of lying on the floor, sobbing, reading, and rereading her book because it quelled my fear that I was losing my mind. Wherever Elizabeth is, I send her my deepest thanks.

I hope my story might be of help to someone else, but I want to make a point that goes right to the heart of the life journey. Other people's journeys are just that—their journeys. They are not my journeys—and my journey is not anyone else's journey. I'm sharing things I believe are true; otherwise, I wouldn't share them. However, I'm not sharing any of this to convince the reader of anything I believe. I want to share things I've tested and practiced that have worked for me. This is my experience.

Understanding the reason for illness and other so-called bad things is of utmost importance to many people. If something has been defined as bad, such as chronic illness, by our traditions, it's a human desire to know why it's happening to us as opposed to someone else. Through my journey, I've learned that the reason for my illness is that my soul chose to *explore* physical reality through the framework of my particular life circumstances, including chronic illness.

Some spiritual communities don't recognize this definition. They say the only worthy outcome of a spiritual and holistic journey is to have, be, and do anything we want. We will always find a parking spot at the mall if we say the right affirmations, think the right thoughts, have enough faith, change the vibratory frequency of our auras, and take the right herbs and homeopathic remedies.

I now know that point of view doesn't work for me. I may have expected health as the result of my healing journey, but what I found was my Self—that larger encompassing me that includes all that I am, human and divine. In finding Self, I also found freedom, which allowed me to move onto something that does work for me. I no longer believe I have failed at life because I have chronic illness. I am still sick, but I have arrived at a place where my heart really understands joy and gratitude.

I reached the conclusions that I have through some rather unusual spiritual paths, as well as through my professional involvement in the disability rights and independent living movements for several decades. Those forces have intertwined throughout my adult life to converge and focus my experiences, consciousness, and energies in a very particular way. That's what I am sharing through my writing.

There is no sense of final achievement in anything I want to share. The journey for me continues every day, moment by moment. It is the consciousness, and finally the acceptance, that this is my reality—for now—that make my life work.

CHAPTER 1

A New Normal

Being generous often consists of simply extending a hand. That's hard to do if you are grasping tightly to your righteousness, your belief system, your superiority, your assumptions about others, your definition of normal.

—Patti Digh[2]

I grew up in the fifties and sixties believing that chronic illness and disability were things to be ashamed of—a belief that was an irony of such magnitude for my future that I could never have imagined it. The person who was affected by them was to be pitied, feared, or scorned, depending on the type of condition. However I looked at it, they were tragedies, and the person had less value in my mind in the scheme of life because of it. It wasn't something I was conscious of though. It was one of those cultural beliefs that I had absorbed from the world around me.

We had a paperboy when I was an adolescent who was described to me as "retarded." No one ever said that he had a disability, but it was evident that there was something different about him. He was a little bit older than I was, and I was afraid of him because he would creep slowly up the driveway, scanning the windows and doors to see if anyone was watching before he would quietly leave the paper by the side door. When he came to collect payment each month, he never said a word. He would stand by the door until someone noticed him. He seemed to be more afraid of me than I was of him.

Another person I knew was treated for mental illness. One day, she was involuntarily committed to the state hospital because she was found wandering down her street without clothes. We talked about her in hushed tones. It was scandalous to say the least. I had a great deal of sympathy for her and how this turn of events would affect her, but I had no understanding of the experience she was going through.

I did know what it was like to live with someone who had the disease of alcoholism and the mental, physical, and emotional issues that it produced. My adoptive mother began losing control over her drinking when I was about eight years old. I felt shamed as a result of her behavior, but I rarely discussed it with anyone—even with friends who were witness to it. I was convinced my mother could stop drinking if she really wanted to. But by the time I was a young adult, I had grown to fear her because of her temper and unpredictability. I despised her because of her abusive and controlling behavior. She died when I was twenty-nine from the effects of cirrhosis of the liver. After her death, it was several years before I was able to put her illness into a context of disability and realize that she was doing the best she could.

In college, there were two women who had obvious physical disabilities. They were the first people I remember meeting with visible disabilities. They were both open and friendly, but I was affected by the same awkwardness that many people are faced with when they meet someone who is disabled: I didn't know how to act or what to say. I may have lost out on potential friendships with them.

Even though I showed signs of immune dysfunction from an early age and have been sick in one way or another my whole life, I did not think of myself as a person with a disability until decades later.

The irony about my early judgment of people with disability and chronic illness is on two counts. The first is that I ended up working in the disability field. Second is that I realized my chronic illness had many things in common with the disabilities I was familiar with in my work. The career choice happened by accident soon after completing my undergraduate studies. My initial entry into the realm of disability was in the field of vocational rehabilitation. This was not a planned career, but a job I fell into because I learned about it through family connections.

I had a degree in sociology with an emphasis in social work, but I knew almost nothing about the needs of people with a wide range of disabilities. Soon thereafter, I completed my graduate studies in counseling with an emphasis in vocational rehabilitation, but I still knew little about the true handicapping factors in our communities. It was several years before I understood that it usually wasn't the individual's disability that was the barrier to participation. It was more often the cultural attitudes about disability that kept the physical and program barriers of social convention in place and prevented employment and inclusion.

Vocational rehabilitation is a government program available to eligible individuals with a disability that can be documented as causing a handicap to achieving employment. Its mission is to prepare people for employment and assist them in obtaining and maintaining that employment. After several years in that field, I found my way into the independent living movement, a dramatically different disability arena led by people with disabilities. This move was to have profound consequences on my personal journey with chronic illness.

I have now been part of the independent living movement for more than thirty-five years. It is an excellent match for my worldview and my own needs as a person with a disabling condition. Being part of the world of people with disabilities—who help themselves—rather than being with professionals who are trained to help people with disabilities was a significant aid in learning how to manage my own life more effectively. The independent living movement introduced me to the concept of *empowerment* put forward by all human rights movements. Figuring out what that term meant to me personally has been the heart of my journey.

The Independent Living Program is federally funded by the same Rehabilitation Act that funds the Vocational Rehabilitation Program, but the two programs are quite different. The Independent Living Program was created by people with disabilities to protest the dominant medical, rehabilitation, and institutional systems that many individuals believed were keeping them dependent, isolated, and disenfranchised from the rest of society. Although most of that traditional care was set up with the intention of doing what was best, it grew out of the historical belief that people with disabilities were defective and in need of being fixed. Fixing people was actually a dramatic update from earlier approaches of hiding and sometimes chaining people in attics or cellars—or even killing them because they were considered too much of a burden for society.[3]

The Rehabilitation Act created centers for independent living, which now exist in all fifty states, the District of Columbia, and five US territories.[4] These centers began to give people with disabilities control over their own services, choices, and destinies. Some centers assist with employment, but mostly they assist with the broader issues of integrated community living: affordable housing, transportation, life skills, benefits management, support services such as personal assistance and sign language interpreting for people who are deaf, and removing architectural and program barriers in public and private settings. In a larger sense, they are places of social transformation because they address the social policies and systems that are the real handicapping structures of our society.

Centers for independent living, as defined by the Rehabilitation Act, are required to be largely governed and staffed by people with disabilities. The person who accesses services at a center is in control of those services, unlike in the medical model of services where the client or patient is often acted upon and the so-called professional is considered to know best.[5] The independent-living model grew out of self-help programs and the disability rights movement, which parallels the civil rights movement in many ways. Both of these movements proclaimed that the person whose life is at stake must be at the forefront of change and speak on his or her own behalf. Centers for independent living are about a philosophy of life, not a place to live, and they don't require medical proof that one has a disability before they will provide services. They are not the assisted-living facilities that many people think of when they hear the term *independent living*. They are meeting places to consult with peers and acquire skills, resources, and an understanding of self-determination. People with disabilities now have their own civil rights legislation, the Americans with Disabilities Act, because the Civil Rights Act didn't protect them.

The reason I mention my profession in a discussion about my health is that one of the places I learned some of the most life-altering lessons about what it means to live effectively with chronic illness was from my friends and colleagues who had conditions that were more typically identified as disabilities, including cerebral palsy, spinal cord injuries, head injuries, psychiatric disabilities, deafness, and blindness.

I did not initially become involved with the Independent Living Program because I identified myself as a person with a disability. I was drawn to it because of the social-change nature of the movement. I love deconstructing old ways of thinking and helping birth new ones. Ironically, the independent living movement has been both a place where I felt discriminated against because I didn't have a visible, traditional disability (my invisible condition was looked at with suspicion by some) and a place where I have learned to embrace my chronic illness as a disability and find a path that helped make my life work. It has certainly been a profession that deflated my own prejudices and misconceptions about people with disabilities and chronic illnesses—and with any kind of differences for that matter.

I have had many teachers in different venues, but the independent living movement broadened my vision about what's true and possible when one is living with so-called limitations in a way that no other teacher could. I believe that the independent living and disability rights movements are part of a kind of transition that is happening globally in which masses of people with all sorts of characteristics—historically believed to be inferior, defective, deviant, or abnormal in some way—are waking up to the truth of their worth, power, and purpose. There is a new normal emerging.

During both my undergraduate and graduate studies, I was required to take statistics courses—to my dismay. I enjoyed and did well in most other math subjects in high school and in my undergraduate work, but I was bored by statistics and spent my days in class struggling to pay attention. One day in the undergraduate class, our instructor was explaining a bell curve, which I was familiar with since some teachers in my high school had graded on a curve.

A bell curve is a shape that develops when data of some kind, such as test grades, are plotted on a graph. It's also used to describe the mathematical concept called normal distribution. The curve looks like a bell, although its height and width will vary depending on the type of data you're plotting, and it shows that the data is concentrated in the center and decreases on either side. The bell curve has been used to define what is normal because most people fall somewhere in the middle—no matter what human characteristic you're measuring. I remember the classroom discussion from decades ago not only because of what the instructor said but how he said it. He paused from writing on the chalkboard and looked out the window with a transcendent look on his face. He told us that he couldn't imagine how anyone could work with statistics and not believe in God. He explained how if you plotted the size of every leaf in the forest, the distribution would show up as a bell curve—and that the same is true of everything on Earth that could be measured.

That kind of thinking about the patterns in nature was consistent with my belief in a divine intelligence, but something else dawned on me several years later. Science and medicine had used statistics to define what was abnormal as well as what was normal. For example, if you're in the middle group in terms of IQ, you're normal. If you're at the high end, you're a genius. If you're at the low end, you're abnormal and intellectually disabled (formerly labeled mentally retarded). People with psychiatric, physical, sensory, and cognitive disabilities were all considered abnormal. And certainly having an invisible chronic illness was considered abnormal.

I bought into that way of thinking for a while, but then it no longer made sense to me. I began to wonder why anything that occurs on the planet would not be considered normal. Leaders in the disability rights movement asked this question several decades ago, and they made note of the fact that anyone can become disabled at any time. Disability is no respecter of persons. It's an ordinary fact of life. It is estimated there are approximately fifty-seven million people with disabilities in the United States.[6] That's a significant percentage of our citizens, and as the population ages, that number is going up dramatically.

An even more staggering statistic reported by the Centers for Disease Control and Prevention (CDC) in 2012 is that about half of all adults in the US—117 million people—have one or more chronic health conditions, including heart disease, stroke, cancer, diabetes, obesity, or arthritis.[7]

Fibromyalgia is estimated to affect ten million people in the US.[8] The word fibromyalgia literally means pain in the muscles, tendons, and ligaments. Fibromyalgia is described by some experts as having abnormal (there's that word again) pain perception to things that other people would not find painful. However, pain in the muscles and fibrous tissue is only one part of fibromyalgia. People with the condition frequently experience headaches, migraines, irritable bowel syndrome, insomnia, significant and persistent fatigue, problems with thinking and memory (sometimes called "fibro fog"), painful menstrual periods, balance problems, morning stiffness, depressed or anxious moods, tingling or numbness in hands and feet, and a number of other symptoms. Impaired coordination, cold intolerance, dry eyes and mouth, sensitivity to light, odors, and vibrations, and restless leg syndrome are also not uncommon in people with FM.

Chronic fatigue syndrome, also known as *myalgic encephalomyelitis*, and chronic fatigue and immune dysfunction, is estimated to affect between one and four million individuals.[9] The CDC attributes the range of estimates to the fact that less than 20 percent of people who have CFS have actually been diagnosed. It is not the tiredness that most people are familiar with. It is a debilitating fatigue combined with a host of other symptoms that are not improved by bed rest, which can get worse after physical activity or mental exertion.

People with CFS often function at a substantially lower level of activity than they were capable of before they became ill. Other symptoms can include post-exertion malaise lasting more than twenty-four hours, sleep that fails to refresh, significant impairment of short-term memory or concentration, muscle and joint pain, headaches, tender lymph nodes, and frequent or recurring sore throats. As with FM, there are often other symptoms that may be related to the CFS or simply co-occurring, such as chemical and food sensitivities, chills and night sweats, irregular heartbeat, and shortness of breath.

Approximately 12–16 percent of the population reports multiple chemical sensitivity (MCS), which is also known as hypersensitivity to common chemicals, environmental illness, and toxicant-induced loss of tolerance.[10] That's up to about fifty-one million people in the US. Other research indicates that more than ten million people in the US have actually been medically diagnosed with MCS.[11] MCS is basically sensitivity to everyday chemicals (including such things as perfumes, petrochemicals, pesticides, and cleaning products) at even low levels of exposure. It is not a dislike of odors; it includes various physical reactions that can involve any system of the body and usually affects many of them, including digestive, respiratory, endocrine, immune, central nervous, musculoskeletal, genito-urinary, and reproductive systems. Reactions can include migraines, severe fatigue, irritable bowel syndrome, chronic infections and rashes, coordination problems, breathing difficulties, seizures, and death. Those affected often have reactions to a wide range of substances other than chemicals, including mold, tobacco and wood smoke, medications, and ordinary foods. Recognition of MCS as a legitimate disorder is growing, although some experts continue to believe it really is caused by psychological problems. There is often considerable overlap in FM, CFS, and MCS, but they are distinctly different disorders. Many of us have been diagnosed with more than one of them.

My intent here is not to present a research paper on these health conditions. I am not a researcher or medical expert on FM, CFS, and MCS. I am an expert on my personal experience with health issues that have been labeled FM, CFS, and MCS. There are other resources available to readers who want more statistical and medical detail. Some of them are listed in the resources section. Instead, the point I want to make is that there are substantial numbers of people in the US who are experiencing these conditions. Some people with FM, CFS, and MCS have identified themselves as disabled and been included in the overall disability statistics, but I'm guessing that most people with these conditions do not identify themselves as having disabilities. Instead, they think of themselves as having medical conditions. All disability statistics are moving targets; at best, we can get a general scope of the size of the population in this country. By anybody's count, it's huge.

If all of the people with disabilities and chronic illnesses came out of their respective closets in this country, many might be astounded by the magnitude of the group. And coming out of closets is indeed happening—in droves.

However, what I have come to believe is that even if there were only a handful of people with disabilities and chronic illnesses, it doesn't matter because whether such conditions are experienced by many or few, they are natural. They are mechanisms for a soul's journey on the physical plane—not a failing, a defect, or a punishment. People with disabilities and chronic illnesses are not victims. In making that statement, I am aware that I'm venturing into delicate territory since I have been in an advocacy and educational role for many years. My goal has been changing the behaviors of those who create and perpetuate barriers (including environmental toxicity) to the full participation of millions of people with disabilities and medical conditions. The two things aren't really a contradiction for me, and I will explain as we go along.

Why wouldn't some people on the planet be born with physical differences? Why wouldn't body parts be formed and arranged differently in some people? Why wouldn't some have more sensitive neurological and immune systems than others? Why wouldn't some have different mental faculties or perceive reality differently? Why wouldn't some people experience accidents that result in disabling conditions? The range of things that occur in nature is beyond the capacity of our finite minds to calculate.

There is still a tendency to characterize people with certain types of disabilities as special, which many of the people I know in the disability rights movement find offensive because it makes them feel like a pet or a mascot. What most say makes them feel included in society is to be known as the adults they are—with the same desire for happiness and right to follow their dreams as everyone else.

Working in the disability field for nearly four decades, I have been able to witness measureable changes in our society that reflect the increasing acceptance of disabling conditions as an aspect of diversity. However, some genetic disabilities, such as muscular dystrophy, are still expected to be cured. Many also hold out expectations of a cure for acquired disabilities, such as spinal cord injuries. There are some people who believe all research dollars should be focused on cures, but the disability rights movement and the passage of the Americans with Disabilities Act have made an indelible imprint on our culture, leading many to believe that it's more useful to be able to participate in life *today* in an accessible environment and inclusive society than it is to wait for some uncertain cure in the future. Those with disabilities who focus all their energies on a cure are following their own path, which is as valid as any other path, but while they are pursuing funding and research focused on a cure, they are also benefitting from the work of the disability rights and independent living movements. These social justice efforts have been largely responsible for making the world more livable and functional for people with all sorts of physical and mental abilities.

It seems that those of us with chronic illnesses are playing a bit of catch up because many still expect that conditions labeled as illnesses rather than disabilities should be cured. If one is "sick," it's assumed by many that wellness will follow at some point if one tries hard enough, has enough faith, and finds the right cure. Books and websites on the subject abound, and many of the ones I have read indicate that not only *can* everyone with a chronic illness be cured but they *should* get well. I believe this type of thinking misses the point. I have come to trust that I am already everything that I'm supposed to be, and if the illness exists, there is a reason. I don't mean that I'm being punished or whipped into perfection. I mean that my soul is exploring dimensions on the earth plane that could not be explored in any other way. That doesn't mean that the illness can't or won't be cured. It means that a cure is not necessarily the goal.

CHAPTER 2

A Little Context

*C*rybaby, neurotic, nervous, aloof, hypochondriac, space cadet, quitter, and damaged are all words that have been used at one time or another to describe me. It's been a long time since anyone has called me such things to my face, which is probably because I have stronger boundaries than in the past. But I remember well the journey from there to here as I struggled with an illness I didn't understand, symptoms that affected how I interacted with other people, and an extremely sensitive nature.

No one who knows me has ever known all the details about my health—except for a few doctors who asked me to fill out in-depth questionnaires. Friends and family members have known pieces. Explaining everything is exhausting, and it's not relevant for everyone who knows me to know all the details. Some are very personal, but I've decided to lay them out here more graphically than ever before. Writing about this is part of the journey, but writing this chapter reminds me of my old fears. I don't want to sound like I'm whining or appear as though I think no one has suffered as much as I have. That's a valid concern for many people with chronic illness. We are often considered hypochondriacs and complainers. It's also challenging for someone as private and introverted as I am to think about someone else reading this. I cannot write my story without providing the framework of my health. The context is the foundation that makes clear the process I went through to find my place in the universe. How I became the person I am today is my story.

I am also carrying a lot of other people's stories in my heart—many of them have experienced real discrimination, misunderstanding, lack of acceptance, and dismissal of their symptoms. I've been hearing stories about others with FM, CFS, and MCS for a long time. I still get phone calls or e-mails from people I do not know because they find me through resources that my organization has published or through others who know me. Many of the stories stir deep feelings of compassion and empathy in me, probably because of what I have experienced. I move forward to write this chapter in hopes that it will be of benefit to me for writing it—and to others as a safe space to trust their own experiences.

I was severely anemic by the age of four. I had frequent and serious respiratory infections throughout childhood, triggering the medical response of liberal use of penicillin and sulfa drugs over a period of many years. Beginning with chronic tonsillitis at the age of five and a tonsillectomy at seven, I graduated to bouts of bronchitis, flu, and strep throat. I was hospitalized twice for pneumonia, and it came close to killing me when I was nine. My adoptive mother said the doctor told her if I got pneumonia again, it would be the end of me. I never came down with pneumonia again, but for decades, I frequently experienced serious infections that made me feel fragile and vulnerable.

By the age of fifteen, I was experiencing unexplainable sleepiness and fatigue. I was a sleepwalker for many years and often was unable to wake myself from my stupor. Much to my chagrin, I was a bed wetter until the age of sixteen.

In college, I started having severe sinus headaches, and my menstrual periods became wildly irregular. I spent a night at a friend's home in a room with a water heater with a gas leak and woke up with a severe headache and an overall flu-like feeling. It was my first memory of being so affected by an environmental substance.

I had two experiences the summer before my junior year that told me there was something unusual about the way my muscles worked. After a deep-sea fishing trip and a bicycle trip, I could not get out of bed. The repetitive motions in both activities inflamed my muscles so severely that I couldn't move the body parts without extreme pain. And there was an overall feeling of debilitation and sickness.

By my senior year, I had trouble staying awake. When I didn't have a class, I would go to my dorm room and sleep. It was apparent to me even in those days that sugar was a problem for me. I had an insatiable appetite for it, and I used it to give myself energy. I would come crashing down within a few hours. My heart would race and skip beats, which really scared me. I went to the doctor who had been my pediatrician throughout childhood. I was nineteen, but he spoke to me in parental tones. He told me I was stressed and just needed to relax. I saw a new doctor who said I had an underactive thyroid and prescribed medication.

During those years, I got to know my biological mother (she gave me up for adoption when I was four). She filled in some of the gaps about the years before the adoption. Two weeks before I was born, she fell down a flight of stairs, flipping me in her womb so that my neck was twisted. Her labor was long and hard because of the head rotation. As a baby, I would scream all night and never sleep. At her wits' end, she consulted with a pediatrician who put me on an "elixir of phenobarbital." She also said that I didn't talk until I was three.

The difficulty staying awake continued into my twenties, and it intensified after I got married. I would fall asleep at my desk at work, and on weekends, I would sleep as much as twenty hours per day. It was obvious to me that the birth control pills I was taking had caused the increased problems. Although my doctor disagreed that they could have such an effect, I stopped taking them. Within a month I was back to my normal level of fatigue and sleepiness.

When I was twenty-four, I began to experience chronic nerve and myofascial pain and dysfunction on the right side of my body—precisely where the severest pain had been following the fishing and bicycle trips. The pain covered my entire right side, including my neck, shoulder, arm, hand, groin, buttock, leg, and foot. I developed contractures and limited range of motion in my right shoulder, neck, and hip. In addition to the problem with sugar, I began to notice that I was reacting to a variety of foods. My abdomen was frequently bloated and tender. Chronic diarrhea set in, and it was the second time a doctor told me I just needed to relax.

I began to have severe menstrual cramps and heavy bleeding. For a couple of days a month, I slept in the infirmary at work because I became weak and faint. I would double over in pain, and my doctor told me to take an over-the-counter painkiller and put my feet up.

When I was twenty-nine, I had a new doctor as the result of a move. The doctor found a cyst the size of a grapefruit on my right ovary. Although surgery was scheduled as soon as possible, the cyst burst before the surgery could take place. The pain had often been unbearable, but I bore it because I was operating as a helpless patient who had been told by a doctor to put her feet up.

When the new doctor opened my abdomen, he found that the ovary had been destroyed. He also found one of the worst cases of endometriosis he had ever seen. They pulled the bowels out of the abdominal cavity to scrape the endometrial tissue off the backside. When the new doctor asked me how I had withstood the pain before the surgery, I seethed with resentment toward my previous doctor.

Shortly after the surgery, urination caused intense burning. The doctor found no infection and referred me to a urologist. The urologist decided I had a constricted urethra and performed a urethrotomy. If I thought urinating had burned before, that procedure gave new meaning to that bodily function.

Many years later, I learned that interstitial cystitis, which is an inflammation of the bladder without an infection, often occurs with FM, CFS, and MCS. Since the burning continues to come and go, depending on what I've eaten or what chemicals I've been exposed to, I ultimately came to believe that the burning was related to toxins my body was clearing out.

Seven years later, the condition returned. I had a second surgery for endometriosis. The surgeries were years before the development of less invasive laser surgery, and I now have painful abdominal adhesions. I finally became pregnant after the second surgery, but I miscarried three weeks later. I experienced infertility throughout my childbearing years and was never able to have the child I longed for. Ultimately, though, menopause put an end to my menstrual difficulties.

Around 1981, I began to have muscle pain and sensitivity to touch all over my body. My doctor immediately checked for arthritis, but those tests came back negative. He didn't know what to recommend except ibuprofen and rest. I also had my second experience with noticeably reacting to chemicals.

That spring, I went to a nursery to pick up some tomato plants. I was standing at the cash register at the front of the store, and I suddenly began to have a peculiar taste in the back of my throat. It tasted like what fertilizer smells like, but we weren't anywhere near the fertilizer shelves. I told the cashier about it, and I was taken aback when she said they were unloading fertilizer at the back of the store. She told me I was probably a sensitive individual and should get out of the store that instant. I took my plants and went home, pondering what had just happened.

I began to notice that when I walked into malls and certain types of stores, my eyes would start burning. I would feel dizzy, disoriented, and confused. My home was treated for carpenter ants, and my ear reacted with such severe pain that I had to sleep in a tent in the yard for two weeks. The exterminator claimed that the chemical he used was safe and couldn't possibly have caused such a reaction.

Cleaning products (especially anything petroleum-based) cigarette smoke, personal care products, cosmetics, and insecticides all affected me significantly. I began to notice and feel nauseous from the formaldehyde that was outgassing from some of my furniture. It sometimes felt like my brain was turning to mush. I began to have difficulty focusing and retrieving words. I developed a chronic bronchial cough, and I was referred to an allergist who did a comprehensive battery of tests. He diagnosed asthma and allergies to a wide variety of substances. Years later, another doctor labeled it reactive airway disease.

I heard about chemical sensitivities as a medical condition and started to remember the heavy chemical load of my childhood in Mississippi. Mosquito trucks sprayed my neighborhood with now-banned DDT during the summers, and we liberally sprayed pesticides to kill the roaches in our house. It was my job to wax our hardwood floors, and I would crawl around on the floors to spread the petroleum-based wax, unmindful of the concept of good ventilation. Our floor furnace, space heaters, and kitchen stove were powered by natural gas. When the doors and windows were closed in the wintertime, the smell hung in the air. My parents were both heavy smokers, and the house was constantly filled with smoke or its residue.

All these memories began to come back to me. I tried to analyze where I might have developed such sensitivity to chemicals and other environmental substances. I thought that my sensitivity had to be the result of an event or a series of events. I hadn't yet thought about the overall lifelong immune dysfunction and its possible role in such reactions.

In 1992, I discovered that a doctor who specialized in environmental illness was within driving distance. I began to consult with her. She conducted tests that no other medical practitioner had ever tried. She identified mineral deficiencies and microbes that were out of control in my body. We worked together for a few years, and I thought I was on to something.

In 1993, I went through a divorce. It was the most stressful time I'd ever been through. The grieving process intensified my symptoms. The fatigue and brain fog became so debilitating that I wasn't sure I could keep working. Many days, I fell into bed at six o'clock after eating dinner, and I didn't get up for twelve hours.

In 1996, I no longer had a choice. Construction materials that outgassed chemicals from renovations at my place of employment tipped me over the edge. I was so fatigued and spacey, I couldn't focus or remember things well enough to manage the heavy responsibilities I carried. I would start crying in the middle of meetings and was irritable and short-tempered. My coworkers didn't understand, and I was too unfocused and fatigued to explain. I felt like a mess. I decided the healthiest choice I could make was to resign. The loss of employment also meant the loss of health insurance. I pretty much gave up going to doctors, although I occasionally allowed myself massage therapy, which I found comforting. I was not eligible for benefits, and I began living off of the small retirement fund I had accumulated.

For four and a half years, I worked at home. I started a mail order business and offered books on chronic illness, specializing in MCS and other emerging illnesses. I ran one ad in an MCS publication and began to get calls from all over the world. Most of the calls were not for book orders. Most of them were from people with chemical sensitivities who were searching for guidance and someone to talk to. I got calls from people who were suicidal. Some wanted help in finding knowledgeable doctors or to share experiences with certain diets or protocols. I wasn't making a living, and the neediness of my customers was more than I wanted to cope with while trying to manage my own illness. I switched to selling music with a focus on healing and spiritual meaning. This decision played a significant role in coming to terms with my life because it brought people around me who reminded me that I was already whole.

In 1999, my house went into foreclosure. I was on the verge of bankruptcy. A relative offered me a rent-free apartment in another state until I could get back on my feet. I moved across several states, and the pieces of my life that felt so broken slowly began to come back together.

In 2000, I was offered a position with an independent living advocacy organization. The director was a friend, and she considered my health condition a disability. She made job accommodations so I could return to work. The office became a fragrance-free zone. I worked in the office three days a week and at home two days a week to help manage my fatigue and reduce my exposure to chemicals. Even with accommodations, it was difficult to work. I was chronically anxious about losing my job.

I had undergone chiropractic manipulations for many years, thinking the pain down the right side of my body was due to a subluxation. I also consulted with an orthopedist, a neurosurgeon, and an osteopathic physician with no relief. Many years later, I learned about chronic myofascial pain and its frequent co-occurrence with fibromyalgia.

In 2001, I developed shingles. When I saw that the lesions were clustering on the fifth cervical vertebra and across my neck, shoulder, arm, and groin precisely where the pain had been all those years, I wondered if the herpes zoster virus had some connection to that historical pain. In fact, the shingles lesions that spread down my right arm wrapped in almost the exact pattern as my childhood chicken pox scars. Perhaps the pre-birth injury to my cervical vertebra provided a fertile environment for the virus to hang out. One chiropractor believes that is likely.

In recent years, I've learned about numerous studies and clinical trials that link chronic fatigue syndrome and fibromyalgia to traumatic neck injuries. Some data strongly suggests that trauma of some kind, especially an injury to the cervical spine, is a precipitating factor.

In 2002, I was offered a position with another independent living organization several states away. They also viewed my health condition as a disability and were willing to make accommodations for me. Although I left that state in 2008 to move back near family, I still work for that organization from home. I have control over my environment, and I have the option to rest when I need to. I travel for work five or six times a year. I generally come home feeling worse than when I left, but I have discovered ways to make the trips manageable most of the time—and I have strategies for extricating myself when I can't.

In 2004, I decided to have the amalgams taken out of my mouth. Although the safety of dental mercury is still controversial, I was persuaded by the literature I had read that it could be a toxic factor in FM, CFS, MCS, and a variety of other health conditions. I felt it was worth doing. However, I was not knowledgeable at the time about a proper detox protocol, and it was not until recently that I tried such a protocol. I've also recently undergone additional dental reconstruction to remove the remaining metal in my mouth.

After the acute episode of shingles in 2001, I have continuously had chronic lesions scattered across my body and in my mucous membranes. I continue to have bouts of post-herpetic neuralgia (nerve pain) over much of the right side of my body. When the virus began surfacing in my mouth, nose, and ears, I developed chronic congestion and a quaky, hoarse voice. Recently, I have hearing loss in my left ear.

In 2005, a clinic specializing in fibromyalgia and chronic fatigue syndrome opened near me. After a comprehensive workup (with more unusual lab tests), they diagnosed the FM and CFS. Between that clinic and the naturopathic doctor I was consulting, I spent about ten thousand dollars in six months, which wasn't covered by insurance. The lab tests indicated high levels of Epstein-Barr virus, cytomegalovirus, other microbes, and almost no natural killer cells (a part of our innate immune system) in my body, which apparently were not uncommon findings. One of the treatments was a medication to deal with those viruses and the shingles virus. It made me too ill to work, and since it cost eight hundred dollars a month—and my insurance company was refusing to pay for it because it was considered experimental—it didn't make sense for me to continue taking it. I was determined not to debilitate myself further or risk the brink of bankruptcy again. I stopped going to the clinic. The clinic went out of business shortly thereafter.

Since then, in spite of having access to some skillful health practitioners, much has continued the same as before. However, my current protocols for toxic metal detox and eliminating microbes are showing promise, so I plan to continue them as long as seems reasonable. Looking at the complex picture retrospectively certainly helps me understand why it's difficult for many people to accept these conditions as physically real. FM, CFS, and MCS are rather mysterious conditions, but they are now more readily identified and treated by the growing number of practitioners who specialize in them. The only plausible thing in the experience of most people in the earlier years was that these had to be mental illnesses, and that many of the symptoms were imagined.

I knew that what I was experiencing was real, but until 2005, depression and despair were central threads in my life. I spent many years feeling disoriented and out of sync with the universe. People around me made little sense to me. I couldn't shake the feeling that I was damaged and being punished by God. I was confused about why I hadn't been healed. I was angry with doctors, family members, and colleagues who didn't understand or believe me. I was full of self-loathing. I had wanted to die for as long as I could remember. I often thought about ending my life because all I could think about was going to sleep for a long time to end the crushing fatigue and escape the unhappiness.

CHAPTER 3

Lists and Things— Let's Get Real

One of the reasons I struggled in my quest to find healing was because of the endless list of things I felt called upon to perfect. I had bought into the belief that humans must juggle a complicated assortment of things in order to have value. I felt required to be godlike, moral, an A-student, superwoman, a productive employee, environmentally responsible, charitable, well-liked, respected, politically correct, a pristine housekeeper, and vibrantly healthy. I was sure that God and the world would judge me about how well I was progressing with the list.

I heard messages all around me that I must be compassionate, caring, gracious, friendly, outgoing (even when I felt awful), consistent, willing, and hardworking. I should allow myself time off only if I'd *really* earned it, have the right body weight and proportions, and be accurate with my words. I should be prosperous, save my money, and be generous with the starving children, homeless people, whales, abused dogs, and victims of every hurricane and tornado. I should recycle plastics, paper, glass, and cardboard, and vote in every election. I must eat the right diet. When they get that figured out, I'd like a share of the profits. I must be on time—even if getting myself ready to go somewhere is exhausting.

I was supposed to be courageous, become a master of mind over matter, and overcome my disability. If I wasn't a poster child, I shouldn't expect to inspire other people, which is the only reason I was born. I shouldn't forget to have healthy self-esteem while doing all of this. If I didn't love myself, it would show to others.

It wasn't acceptable to lack confidence, carry shame, or be self-sabotaging. I should sparkle, my eyes should dance, and my hair should shine. As a student of the metaphysical, I should always be manifesting everything my heart desires into reality: attracting the mate of my dreams, healing the sick, winning the lottery, or building my mansion.

I just wanted to crawl in a hole, and I often wanted to die. I kept trying to live up to spiritual ideals and social acceptability because I wanted to earn the goodwill of the Divine and friends, family, and colleagues. My heroes had been the long-suffering saints who endured any amount of pain and misery that was presented to them—cheerfully and always with more concern about other people than themselves. Somewhere along my path, I had come to believe that was required.

The books I read and gurus I listened to all had beautiful, logical things to say. Why weren't they resolving my issues? I tried to sort out how to apply the philosophies and theories of healing that I was reading about, but I felt inept and discarded by the universe. Part of my discouragement came from the realization that none of the improvements to myself were making me well. The rest of my discouragement came from thinking that if no greater wellness was forthcoming, there must be something wrong with me. I concluded that I was being punished for not getting it right. I bounced back and forth between "I screwed up" and "I am screwed up." I made too many mistakes, did not work hard enough, and was not an adequate human being.

I was struck by how one new age thought bewildered me. Many of the authors I consulted talked about life becoming easy if you envisioned it being easy, set your intention for everything to fall into place, and learned to go with the flow. I understood the spiritual principles of coming into the present moment, being more conscious of what I was feeling and observing, and not getting attached to the outcome of what I was asking for, but I still found most of my life challenging. It seemed that I couldn't even get that right.

Eventually, it dawned on me: living with serious chronic illness *isn't* easy. Those who claim it *should* be easy, although they've never lived with chronic illness, don't know what they're talking about. It didn't get any easier until I owned up to the fact that it wasn't easy. That's when I started dealing with the reality of it.

The complexities overwhelmed me for years. The conflicting advice about proper diet and the right nutritional supplements kept me on a dizzying merry-go-round. Macrobiotic, alkaline, food-rotation, high-protein, specific-carbohydrate, food-combining, salicylate-free, grain-free, carbs-protein-fats in a particular ratio, and anti-inflammatory diets were recommended. They were substantially different from each other, but they all required a considerable amount of planning and coordination. One expert would say we should eat more of a particular food because of the high content of certain nutrients. Another would tell us to never eat that particular food because it was high in something toxic or had chemicals that could potentially interfere with the absorption of nutrients. Every recommendation had an opposing point of view.

Are these conditions the result of psychological, neurological, hormonal, or immunological factors? Or is it all of the above? It depends on whom you're listening to. Damaged detoxification pathways, autoimmune disease, inflammation, neurological damage, trauma, MTHFR gene mutation, adrenal insufficiency, rampant microbes, defective mitochondria, cellular agglutination, vitamin and mineral deficiencies, heavy metal poisoning, overly acidic body pH, and many other causes and factors are all bound to come up in a search for answers.

The numbers of therapeutic regimens that are recommended fill volumes. And practitioners seem to emphasize something different at different times. This week, it might be magnesium and malic acid. Next week, it might be transfer factors, methyltetrahydrofolate, phosphytidalcholine, guaifenesin, or numerous other substances that most of us have never heard of—or can even pronounce. Enzymes, amino acids, glandular formulas, vitamin B12, vitamin C, probiotics, and a long list of other nutrients became a part of my everyday language. My desire to be well sent me off in contradictory directions, crisscrossing and stopping and starting because I felt so engulfed by information.

With my food sensitivities, meal planning can be complicated. Eating out is a significant challenge. In the early days of trying to cope with my body's reactions to such a wide variety of foods, I was operating out of such a sense of shame for the peculiarity of my problem that I would not speak up and request the kind of foods I needed. When I revealed my sensitivities, my dietary constraints would become the subject of dinner conversation, causing me considerable discomfort.

For one Thanksgiving celebration, I did not tell the hostess ahead of time, thinking that I would find enough to eat out of the anticipated spread. It turned out there was only one thing on the vast table that I could eat. The only skills I had at my disposal at the time were pouting and withdrawing. It was the first time I realized how much food was tied to my sense of being loved and nurtured. The negative reaction from others at the table intensified my feelings of shame and chastisement. As with every other thing that has occurred with this illness, there was a benefit to going through that experience. I started to learn self-advocacy skills around food that made me a stronger self-advocate overall.

Many of us started the journey with FM, CFS, and MCS with the instruction to heal the yeast overgrowth, which is common when the immune system has broken down. As we pursued treatments, we discovered a vast array of medications, supplements, diets, and routines that were all thought to be the solution. Then came an emphasis on parasites, removing all chemicals from our environments (not totally possible), tending to our leaky guts, underlying viruses, and bacteria, cleansing our colons, flushing our livers, strengthening our immune systems, removing dental amalgam and other metals from our mouths, eliminating all foods in the nightshade family or those containing salicylates, and replacing our deficient hormones and missing enzymes. The more I listened and researched, the more complicated, expensive, and exhausting it seemed.

I used to think that the only thing worse than living with a multiplicity of symptoms was reading about those symptoms in some book that offered myriad treatments for all those symptoms. I was supposed to choose, implement, keep track of, and often deal with the side effects of them (while managing fatigue and pain).

Some people have been healed by the approach they recommend in their books. The testimonials are intriguing and persuasive. It was my belief that what worked for another would work for me. That thought propelled me through several decades. I thought the answer was right around the next corner.

Coming up against the limits of my pocketbook has been the reality checkpoint at several junctures. Insurance doesn't cover a lot of the treatments for FM, CFS, and MCS since they generally include expensive organic and nonallergenic foods, body work (massage and other therapies), eliminating chemicals from our environments (a costly undertaking when you realize chemicals are in most things, including the materials used to construct your house, furniture, mattress, and electronic devices), and large amounts of nutritional supplements. Some traditional medications are often covered by insurance, but like many others with these disorders, I don't tolerate drugs well. The first time I left a practitioner's office after spending four hundred dollars on nutritional supplements, I had a foreshadowing of things to come.

When I went back to work, the illness continued to have a significant impact on my finances. I was convinced that a cure was imminent—and that I should be cured—and I was willing to keep pouring money into the next promising treatment.

At various points, I have had ample resources in income and insurance to explore some of the most highly acclaimed treatments and protocols. At other times, I have had virtually no resources to try anything.

Some of the practices I tried made me feel that I was gaining some control over my life. In those instances, the *process* made me feel more whole; taking responsibility for my own health and making my own choices were empowering. I found a book about healing yeast overgrowth that was so persuasive in its arguments that I adopted it wholeheartedly. I was so determined to follow the author's guidance that I got up early every morning and walked for an hour (as she suggested) after willing my leaded arms and legs to get out of bed. I followed her diet religiously—in spite of the fact that it intensified my hypoglycemia. I stumbled through months of being chronically hungry, losing weight from my already slender frame, and jumping through hoops to prepare the required foods while managing a job and a home. (I finally concluded that the book's author must be unemployed.)

Maintaining that lifestyle when I was so fatigued was grueling, I could hardly focus on anything else. But I later realized that the psychological effect of disciplining myself to maintain the protocol strengthened my skills in taking charge of my own life, which I had not learned as a child.

Once it became clear that the protocol was not healing my body—and was diminishing my well-being—I abandoned the approach. The unintended (but welcome) result of sharpening my will had been enough. To this day, I am thankful for that experience. Learning lessons does not have to be painful or a struggle, but until we know that, experiences like this can be great teachers.

There are numerous other issues that have been a part of my experience throughout the years. Some readers may wonder whether I tried this or that type of treatment and what experience I had with it. I tried many things over several decades, but the main story I want to share is not the medical journey I took. My spiritual journey is what matters most to me.

What I came to understand over the next few years was that one of the most important aspects of my journey was trusting myself and hearing my inner guidance about choices that are right for me as a unique individual—whether it's medical treatments to choose from, activities to engage in, beliefs to introduce into my value system, or priorities to set for my time and energy. The opinions of the medical and spiritual experts are things that I can consider, and I have come to have deep appreciation for the contributions that so many of them have made to the body of knowledge. But on a day-to-day basis, I get to choose how I dance with the illness and with my life.

The lists of things to do and perfect that had loomed so large in the first decades of my life turned out to be nothing more than grist for the mill. They had only the meaning that I gave them. I started to learn what it meant to get real and accept that I could only give as much as I had to give. If I kept trying to perfect something that couldn't be perfected—and give what I didn't have to give—I would keep driving myself deeper into a hole.

CHAPTER 4

Exiting the Game

Why is it so much easier to believe in victims, randomness, chaos, evil, win-lose scenarios, humans being powerless or weak little beings at the mercy of forces beyond our control than it is to believe in choice, purpose, intelligence, power, planning, and tremendous benefit for all involved?
—Robert Scheinfeld[12]

Truman Burbank, the character played by Jim Carrey in *The Truman Show*, had no inkling that his whole life had been a reality TV show from the day he was born. His daily activities were conducted on a stage that appeared to be a real community and televised to the whole world. Everyone around him was invested in keeping him ignorant of his true identity because no one wanted to lose the emotional connection to the people they'd grown so attached to on screen. In essence, Truman's life was produced and directed by someone other than himself. By the end of the story, Truman discovered the truth. With some difficulty, he found the exit off the stage. When he opened the door, all we could see was darkness. There was no knowing what was on the other side, but Truman walked through the door courageously to claim his life—in whatever form it was to take.

In 2005, I found what I believed to be my exit door. I didn't completely walk through the door, but I opened it and peered into the darkness on the other side. After a while, I began to take baby steps into a strange new realm. I started learning how to play a different game than the one I had believed was the only choice I had. It was one of the biggest shifts in my process. I began to embrace the belief that chronic illness is a soul journey. I began to understand that I hadn't failed as a human being or as a spiritual quester because I was sick. I was not a victim of the failings of doctors, parents, authors, the chemical industry, and everyone else I was blaming. After years of working in the disability rights arena—where it is believed that disability is an ordinary life experience, not a tragedy—I finally understood that chronic illness is the same.

From that realization, the most immediate change that took place was learning that the depression and suicidal thoughts I had experienced were a totally separate issue from the FM, CFS, and MCS. Depression is often listed as one of the symptoms of those illnesses, and some practitioners use it to justify diagnosing FM, CFS, and MCS as psychological in origin. It is not a separate issue for everyone. A deficiency of certain nutrients and other chemical reasons that are often a part of FM, CFS, and MCS can lead to depression. But my experience was that I started to understand just how much power I had over my thoughts.

One day when I was contemplating suicide again and searching the Internet to find ways to kill myself, I began to laugh at myself. I found myself speaking out loud, saying, "If you really want to kill yourself, you have a right to do it; but please go ahead and do it, because if you're not going to do it, shut up about it!"

I wasn't beating myself into submission. I was underscoring the point so that I would take my new perspective seriously. I did shut up about it for the most part. There have been a few times since that year when it has crept into my thoughts again, but each time, I have chosen not to go there. It's not an act of will so much as it is a shift in consciousness about what I have control over. When I stopped feeling like a victim, many other things came into focus.

The depression lifted, but the physical issues were still there. I began to understand the difference between depression and malaise —another odd word that we often hear ascribed to FM, CFS, and MCS. The definition of malaise is as vague as is the experience of it. Recognizing the distinction, however, was a breakthrough. Understanding that I could feel fatigued, lethargic, and uncomfortable physically wasn't the same thing as believing that I was worthless and that life was hopeless. Stopping my tendency to bundle everything I was experiencing into one overwhelming ball was an early key to starting to make my life work.

Since 2005, I have continued to try various approaches to getting well. Some things have helped, and others have made me sicker. This is a common experience for many people with FM, CFS, and MCS since the causes and symptoms vary from person to person. But what has characterized my experience with the illness since that time has been that the search for a cure became secondary to my changing perspective about the *meaning* of the illness. I came to understand that I am much larger than my illness, and that there is nothing wrong with me as a human being or as a soul because I have an illness. I reached a different kind of understanding of the purpose of life.

The idea that experiencing chronic, life-threatening, or terminal illnesses and psychiatric or physical disability means there is something wrong with us has been a part of our cultural and religious definitions for thousands of years. This definition arose from the foundational belief that all reality must be classified as good or bad and right or wrong, and should or shouldn't be the way that it is.

I believe we have entered an era in history in which another way of looking at reality has revealed itself. I like to think of life on Earth as a soul's opportunity for exploration and creativity now rather than a test of my worthiness that is required so that I can earn and learn my way into the graces of God. I no longer believe that we're being punished or rewarded for being sick or getting well because I no longer see sickness as bad and wellness as good. I no longer think that I did something wrong or chose the wrong course of action because I'm not healthy. I now describe chronic illness as annoying, uncomfortable, and challenging, which brings a different quality to my life than the word *bad*.

I now see the human experience within a hierarchical framework that all of our souls had a role in designing—as a game, a way for Spirit to play with time and space and limits and boundaries. In a hierarchical world, judgment is essential, even required, to fully participate. Everything that exists must be classified as good, better, best, bad, worse, or worst. Each classification is better than or worse than another classification. Everything is either right or wrong, and it should or shouldn't be the way that it is.

There is a hierarchy of race, gender, sexual orientation, darkness or lightness of skin color, income, economic status, occupation, military and corporate rank, physical and mental abilities, body size, height, physical attractiveness, school grades, education, makes of automobiles, neighborhoods, marital status, and level of health in the physical realm. If you are a poor, uneducated woman of color who is a lesbian, who uses a wheelchair, and has a mental illness, you have a boatload of adventures facing you in a hierarchical game.

In a hierarchy, there are few shades of gray. Everything is gauged according to whether or not you get the right product in the end. If you're sick, the appropriate end product is to get well. Even the new age movement, which changed up the game a bit, tells us that we should be creating a better reality than the one we've created. I had moved from a traditional religious point of view that I was inadequate because I hadn't found enough faith to be cured to a new age principle that I should be manifesting my dreams and attracting all the reality I wanted. I continued to judge myself when I was still sick.

I have come to believe that hierarchical, judgmental thinking has power over us until we recognize it for what it is. The process of recognizing our inherent worth, regardless of any physical, mental, emotional, behavioral, or economic characteristic, has been unfolding for several decades as we are coming into alignment with our soul selves, and opening our minds and societal structures to equality, human rights, and personal empowerment.

I believe we are experiencing a shift in consciousness, a sort of transition on Earth. This option is increasingly available to humans. We are beginning to play a different game than the one we've been playing for eons: the Divine masquerading as human beings. Instead of framing our identity as physical beings with spirits, a growing number of us are embracing the idea that we are more precisely spiritual beings having physical experiences.

Transition suggests moving from one place to another. I don't know where it's leading. I just believe it's an option. It's not because the game is bad, but some of us are tired of playing it and wish to do something else. Learning how to leave the hierarchical game and letting go of expectations, rules, customs, and beliefs that no longer serve us can be extremely challenging when that has been your whole world. Our behaviors, language, feelings, and societal structures are all rooted in a deep and ancient agreement about what a human is and how we prove our worthiness. Knowing that we are already divine ends that notion and offers a different framework for the purpose of living.

As my understanding of life as exploration rather than a test deepened, I started to see that everything I had ever experienced was an opportunity—not metaphorically, but mechanically. The concept of opportunity is not offered as a feel-good, psychological term for the purpose of manipulating anyone's perceptions. It's offered as a definition of how I believe life works: a situation or circumstance showed up, and this is the opportunity in it. With that shift in perspective, I realized that every seemingly hurtful, uncomfortable, unfair, and unjust thing that had ever happened to me was simply a tool I could use to open doors that I didn't know existed before.

As my writing progresses, I will share some of the transitional understanding that has come to me in the past decade.

CHAPTER 5

Metaphysics, Magic, Medicine, and Mumbo Jumbo

B eing a new age junkie, I was an avid reader of self-help, holistic health, and spiritual growth concepts. I devoured hundreds of books in search of healing solutions for my health issues. I set up expectations that I would be cured because of how passionately I believed that would come to pass. Many of the books I read seemed to say it was possible by following their plans. The net result was that I ended up feeling like a spiritual failure when my health didn't improve.

Three of the concepts that I played with (and was greatly confused by) were affirmations to manifest what I wanted, creating my own reality, and the law of attraction.

My feeling of failure was the result of two things. Sometimes I accepted without question an expert's suggestion that I *could* and *should* be able to cure myself with a particular approach. Other times, I was filtering the material through the lens of good or bad, right or wrong, and should or shouldn't. There might not have been any inference in the writings that I should get well, but because I categorized illness as a bad thing, when I realized I was still sick, I felt like a failure.

Saying affirmations and consciously choosing to think positive thoughts can be helpful tools for many people at certain times. Our beliefs and feelings are reflected in our language. Making a conscious effort to change negative thoughts and emotions through reversing our thoughts and words can be a powerful tool for change.

I was confused because I believed there was something magical about affirmations and positive thinking that would result in fixing everything in my life that I didn't like. I meandered with those ideas for a number of years until I was no longer sure what was real, what I was conjuring up, what I was attracting, why it was happening to me, and why people didn't believe I was sick. I created a kind of insanity that some people were accusing me of. Then I found myself in a frightening situation. Because I believed I had "attracted" something into my life, I thought I was supposed to stay with it and just love the people involved and all would be sublime. What I needed to do, and finally did, was get out of the situation.

I realize that the explanation of the law of attraction is not as straightforward as what I understood it to be at the time, but it didn't matter when I was so unhappy. Even what I had been taught about God's love for me couldn't trump my feelings of being defective and punished because I was chronically sick. It seemed that the very act of trying to create the reality I wanted meant there was something wrong with the reality I had.

I've noticed people in abusive situations who struggle with the concept of the law of attraction. They interpret it as meaning that if they're being treated disrespectfully, it's because their energy attracted the behavior and they deserve it. They think they're being punished for their supposed failures. Many people interpret chronic illness and disability in this way also. Some see it as God's judgment. Others see it as karmic payback.

An unusual application of the law of attraction that I witnessed was the interpretation that disability organizations shouldn't be given money because people with disabilities were not experiencing anything that they had not summoned unto themselves. The people with disabilities I talked to about that interpretation assumed that the person believed that if you had a disability, you were being punished in some way—and that was why you shouldn't be given assistance. We don't know that for sure, but the person's opinion is definitely a curiosity. Just because we are all souls who play roles in our circumstances, does it necessarily follow that we shouldn't help and support one another?

One person explained that the concept of creating your own reality meant that if I decided I wanted to be the president of Argentina, I could make that happen by following the principles found in popular literature. The viewpoint raised a serious question for me. Would the Argentinian people elect a US-born woman to be their president even though it's against their constitution to do so? I would have to be an exceptionally adept master of metaphysical laws to pull that off, which I am not. And it doesn't necessarily follow that someone who is a master could overturn the Constitution of Argentina by manipulating the will of its citizens. This example may seem far-fetched, but it's not much different from other expectations I had set up around various aspects of my life, including chronic illness. If I wanted to cure myself or be wealthy or acquire fame, I could just affirm those things into being.

I wove an integrated bubble of old-fashioned faith and my new beliefs about creating the reality I wanted. As I applied a multitude of healing modalities and believed with all my heart that I would be cured, I had some success with manifesting some of the other things I wanted. However, I continued to be sick. It was as if I had accomplished nothing at all. I continued to believe there must be something wrong with *me*.

Barely a day goes by that I don't hear someone on television say, "Anything is possible." I hear it from sports figures who break records, people who are in remission from cancer, and musicians who want to hit it big. The concepts of climbing every mountain and wishing upon a star are such integral parts of the way we perceive the world that most of us don't even blink when we hear them. On *Star Trek,* Scotty could rebuild an engine core in thirty minutes—instead of the two days the manual said was necessary.

I started to wonder if I had misunderstood the creating your own reality thing. By the same token, I began to ask, "What if I have misunderstood the faith thing?" If I had enough faith, could I be cured of anything? Was it a matter of just getting into the water? Had all the people who died of cancer—in spite of deep faith—been spiritual failures? What about the scriptural reference that with God all things are possible? I realized I had interpreted that to mean that because all things are *possible,* they *should* happen.

I have heard many people say that the real meaning of creating your own reality has to do with altering my perceptions of reality by changing my thoughts about the meaning of that reality. That has come closer to the truth for me than the other sweeping declaration. If I think of chronic illness as a bad thing, it seems to naturally follow that I'm being punished and that there is something wrong with me that must be fixed. What if chronic illness and disability aren't bad things but simply characteristics for a soul's journey on Earth?

It's difficult to think about illness and disability as things that could bring positive benefits. In fact, chronic illness and disability seem so illegitimate to us that we adopted the use of the word *invalid* to describe the person experiencing it. The word means both "without foundation or force in fact, truth, or law"[13] and (pronounced differently) "sickly." Many people in the disability rights movement have commented on how disempowering they find the phrase *invalid coach*, which is stenciled on some vans.

We have struggled so much with the nature of disability and illness that we have to make people special to process the experience of individuals who are born with certain disabilities or become significantly disabled as a result of injury. We label what happened to them tragedies and make them heroes. We call them courageous beyond comprehension. Those of us who live with disabilities and chronic illnesses on a daily basis know the truth. Most of us are pretty courageous—but not in the sense that's put forward in popular media. Our courage is no more real or holy than the courage of every other person on the planet. We all deal with the realities and limitations of the physical realm. I don't want to be considered a saint because of what I live with, but I do want to be taken seriously.

Should everyone who has a disability, acute illness, or chronic illness be cured because we can't stand to see anyone suffer? Can all of these people be cured by trying harder? Probably not. That is not to say that we aren't creating realities of all sorts every day. We create a great deal with our thoughts and beliefs, which lead to actions and choices that maintain or alter the course of our lives. But creation is often not a straight line between conscious thought or action and outcome. The outcomes and results are often things we did not foresee or consciously choose.

Because we believe all things are good or bad, right or wrong, or should or shouldn't be happening, we almost can't fathom the idea that a soul would voluntarily explore illness or disability. What if some reality is being created by our souls to serve a larger purpose? What if illness and disability are a process of seeking, discovering, and experiencing? How we experience reality when we believe we're being punished or are defective can be quite different from how we experience reality when we believe that we are all that we were meant to be.

The measure of any process in life (illness, relationship, job, financial hardship) is where it takes us. The illness may have no particular meaning, but the specific paths it has taken me down—the things I've learned, the choices I've made, the things I have contributed, many of the people and circumstances that have come into my life—could not have been possible without the chronic illness and its set of characteristics. What if my soul wanted to gain insights about mind-body-spirit-emotions that can only come from living with illness? Participating in a sport is, after all, very different from being a spectator.

Many aspects of our lives and our experiences are created unconsciously or seemingly coincidentally. Learning how to be conscious creators is a process that takes time and practice, and we are not flawed if we haven't yet mastered that skill. What if creating reality is a collaborative effort between my finite human self and my soul? As a physical being and a finite thinker, perhaps I am served in a more useful way when I recognize that I can't necessarily know what is in my best interest. What if success is not just a matter of letting go and letting God? What if it is about being in a genuine partnership with the Divine? In a partnership, the collaborators bring something different to the table. Everyone has different ideas and competencies.

As a finite human, I have a certain level of intelligence, earthly experience, interests, and preferences. My soul has a cosmic view of my purpose and an understanding of how life works mechanically, that I as a finite being do not. Coming into a state of consciousness that allows me to know what my soul knows is a process. Perhaps it is possible to be in sync with my soul by the time my physical body dies. Perhaps I will have power over more of my reality by then.

For now, my reality is that my soul is living in a body that is experiencing physical and mental characteristics that I have not yet been able to end finitely. Operating as a partner with that greater aspect of my being does not negate the act of trusting the Divine. For the partnership to work effectively, I must trust that there are some things I do not know and cannot know. It doesn't mean that I am required to go into a state of mystical oblivion and not have any opinions or preferences. It does mean giving up having to know the reason things have happened the way they have and trying to control the outcome of everything.

It means trusting that my best interest is always the mission of the partnership.

For years, I pursued a variety of spiritual and metaphysical practices in an effort to get well, believing there was something wrong with me. I discovered that prayer, positive thinking, affirmations, meditation, yoga, rebirthing, guided imagery, and a host of other practices could support my physical and mental health. They helped me reconnect body and mind with spirit. They heightened my consciousness of what's true and not true, and they deepened my appreciation for my own worth and the oneness of all that is. They increased my contentment and feelings of stability in the midst of painful and sometimes insane circumstances. They did *not* teach me magic tricks to change all the reality in my world.

My journey has taught me more about recognizing and cooperating with what is real than it has about manifesting what I want. That's my journey; the experience of others may be different. I have not stopped believing in magic. I see magic all around me every day: in a sunset, a new baby, the acts of kindness of friends and strangers alike, and the unending adoration of my dogs and cats. The wonders never cease.

CHAPTER 6

Is It Mind, Body, and Spirit or Mind, Mind, and Mind?

L et's talk about the psychological interpretation of chronic illness for a moment. It's the elephant in the room that many people with invisible chronic illnesses focus on. Many of us have focused so intently on it because a label of mental illness is far more stigmatizing in our culture than labels of chronic illness and physical disability.

Many people with fibromyalgia, chronic fatigue syndrome, chemical and electrical sensitivities, Lyme disease, Crohn's disease, ulcerative colitis, lupus, arthritis, allergies, asthma, migraines, attention deficit disorder, and a number of other conditions are familiar with being told their symptoms are psychological or psychosomatic in origin. Paul Donoghue and Mary Siegel wrote about this phenomenon in *Sick and Tired of Feeling Sick and Tired: Living with Invisible Chronic Illness*. I recommend the book for anyone with invisible chronic illness.

The psychological pronouncements of friends, family members, coworkers, and medical practitioners started me thinking about writing this book several years before I actually started writing it. In my earlier days of working in the independent living movement, I was not considered a person with a disability because I had no easily identifiable signs of a disability, had no disability diagnosis, and had never declared a disability. I was not accepted by a number of people who had more recognizable disabilities. I was directly told on a number of occasions that I had no right to be in the positions I held because I didn't have a disability. I understood that point of view, even though I knew I had an illness. I knew the importance of having someone with an identifiable disability in high-profile positions. The civil rights and women's movements would have never succeeded as they did if Martin Luther King had been white or if women's liberation had been led by a man. The point of a people's movement is to give the people whose lives are at stake control of their own destinies.

As I began to own up to the fact that my own illness was a disabling condition, I started to selectively share my challenges with chemicals and tobacco smoke. I began to receive feedback that some thought my reactions were psychological. I knew that point of view was just reflecting a prevailing belief in our culture. I had heard it before. No one knew the extent of the health issues I was dealing with because I hadn't communicated it. I had been operating out of fear that I would be labeled as someone with a psychological problem, and I had kept most of it to myself.

After experiencing those comments a few times, I started isolating myself. I felt excluded and unwelcome. I disconnected emotionally, and I made a conscious choice to continue withholding information about my health out of fear that I would be labeled mentally ill. I was acutely aware of the prejudice surrounding psychiatric disability. I could just imagine the possible response if I were to start sharing the rest of the information about my chronic fatigue, body-wide pain, food sensitivities, and cognitive issues.

This isn't a criticism of the independent living movement. The people who started the movement had significant visible disabilities and faced barriers that most of us with invisible disabilities weren't dealing with. They were just trying to survive. Since those days, the movement has gained more flexibility with financial and human resources that have expanded its reach. It has grown in its understanding of communities' needs around physical, mental, cognitive, and emotional characteristics, including those that are completely invisible and not yet well understood.

Many centers for independent living and the national membership organizations have instituted policies restricting fragrances, chemicals, and smoking on their property and at their events, as a disability accommodation. Some have taken this step as a human accommodation. Many have started to realize that a chemical- or smoke-laden environment is also harmful to anyone with asthma, allergies, lung disease, heart disease, and other health conditions as well as to humans in general. The Centers for Disease Control, American Lung Association, and others have modeled how policies and procedures can be instituted within an organization that employees and visitors can easily follow.

A funny thing happened to humans on the way to understanding ourselves better: we began a love affair with Freudian psychology that resulted in creating a framework for explaining just about everything through psychological terms. It has been a fun ride. I enjoyed it as much as the next explorer. I fantasized about being a therapist at one time because I was so fascinated by the mind and the role our childhoods play in shaping our feelings about ourselves. Denial, projection, neurosis, resistance, psychosis—and then there's psychosomatic illness.

People with chronic illness don't often hear the term *psychosomatic*. I don't know if it's an unfamiliar term for most people or if we've just gotten so used to using the term *psychological*. Many people don't think about using psychosomatic. When we are told our illnesses are psychological, we often suspect that they really believe they are imaginary. Sometimes they really mean psychosomatic, which means the physical signs and symptoms are real—but they are caused by something like the wear and tear that stress, grief, or anxiety can have on the body. Most people can relate to that definition. We often hear people say, "I've been working too hard—that's why I got this cold."

Whatever people mean by the term when they say it, I'm not sure what I'm supposed to do with someone's declaration that my illness is psychological. Should I put the heating pad on my brain rather than on the body parts that hurt? Should I head for the psychiatrist's office when my knees begin to buckle from fatigue? That kind of hit-and-run profiling has not been useful on a practical level, but ultimately there has been value in the declaration because it spurred me to find my own truth. I deeply resented things that were said to me until I realized such comments were opportunities to take my life in a different direction.

I began my healing journey with the assumption that I needed emotional healing. I knew I had grown up in a challenging family environment. In those days, I was more concerned about my anxiety, depression, and introversion than the recurring infections and fatigue. I saw those things as just recurring; *chronic* never entered my mind. I had some vague notion that I had a weaker immune system than most, but I didn't know there was a term for it. No doctor ever commented on the fact that I had been frequently sick since I was an infant. That seems odd on one level, but I also recognize that it was a valid part of my journey.

I did go for therapy. I believed in psychological counseling then—and I believe in it now. Psychologists and personal coaches supported me through some of my most difficult times. Did it cure me? No, but it helped strengthen my trust in myself and my competencies to better manage my life, including the chronic illness.

Of course stress can affect us and play a role in our health. Our reactions to stress can alter blood pressure, blood sugar, heart rates, and other measureable processes. The research on that is extensive (although not definitive). I have ample evidence that stress can aggravate my symptoms; by the same token, a relaxed, trusting state of mind has not cured me. But stressors are not just psychological factors. Ongoing pain and illness are also neurological stressors that we experience because we have human nervous systems—not because we're defective. It's our interpretation of what the effect of stress means about what we're experiencing, and our adequacy because of it, that becomes a problem. (We will discuss a helpful tool for managing stress in a later chapter.)

As we have explored the psychological realm, many of us began to realize that we had done something rather goofy in that process. We had cut off the psychological aspect of ourselves from everything else. Like the scientist who isolates a virus to study it in the laboratory, we were holding the psychological part of ourselves under a microscope, as if it alone were the answer to all of life's mysteries.

This phenomenon hasn't just affected those of us with physical disabilities and illnesses that are dismissed as psychological. It has also affected people with so-called certifiable mental illness. As a result of the labeling that their condition is psychological, many people with psychiatric disabilities have their physical needs ignored and only their psychological needs attended to.

Because centers for independent living are holistic in their approaches, rather than focusing on a person's diagnosis, they have noticed how lack of coordination between general medical and psychiatric care can be a barrier to recovery and independence. Whether the person's diagnosis is psychiatric, intellectual, cognitive, sensory, or physical, we've observed how health care and rehabilitation systems often divide up authority over specific domains and ignore those factors that are not part of their authority. This kind of splitting off of care happens to people whose primary disability is physical but who have a secondary diagnosis of a psychiatric condition. People with intellectual disabilities can also have diagnoses of physical and/or psychiatric conditions.

The mind part of the body-mind-spirit trinity isn't bigger, more important, or more valid than the other two parts. We are multidimensional beings. If we're making bean soup, we don't serve the beans in one bowl and the water, ham hocks, and salt in another. The ingredients have to be blended together to call it bean soup. Our human-divine nature is a soup. When we think of a symptom or a condition as totally physical or totally psychological or totally spiritual, we miss the blended nature of ourselves—that is, our wholeness. Heart disease, for example, was associated with stress levels for a long time. The focus in some circles was on relaxation therapy and anger management—treatments in the psychological realm. But over time, the equation was balanced with healthier nutrition, preventative checkups, and spiritual practices.

Treating the whole person has moved up the hierarchical ladder of acceptability for many diseases and conditions. Viewing people with FM, CFS, and MCS holistically has been moving up the ladder also. We're not quite there yet, but science is starting to establish that they are measureable physiological phenomena. They may also involve psychological factors of one degree or another.

While this slow process is taking place, we have an opportunity as a society. We can rethink what it means to have a psychological component to humanity. And those of us with chronic illnesses can identify the gift for ourselves in this exploration.

The hierarchical way of thinking about our psychological aspects is no longer necessary. We have believed that depression, anxiety, hallucinations, manic states, worry, fear, and other so-called negative states are bad. Because these things are considered bad, many people have assumed that if we're not thinking happy thoughts every moment and behaving in certain ways, we're unspiritual, damaged, defective, or crazy. Psychological states may cause challenges in acquiring what we *think* we want from our lives, but they do not prevent us from making the journeys our souls are after.

I had many prejudices about people with psychiatric disabilities when I was new to the disability rights arena. When I was a "professional" service provider, I considered myself the expert and the person with the psychiatric diagnosis as the recipient of my wisdom. That, of course, is the issue that the disability rights and independent living movements have been working to change.

One of the best teachers who helped me uncover my own bias was a colleague who had been treated for "mental illness." I hadn't realized that the disability rights movement was considered by some to be as prejudiced as the larger society about psychiatric disabilities. I had believed, like many others, that when someone was "exploring a different reality" (as defined by the psychiatric hierarchy), the only acceptable response was to hospitalize the person, even against his or her will. The colleague explained what it's like to be involuntarily committed to a treatment facility and to be forced to take medications that you know are harmful to you. Even more enlightening was when he explained how the doctor said it was his duty to enforce *his* reality because he had the authority to declare something was wrong with my colleague's reality.

In that moment, a huge part of my own worldview shifted—about people who've been labeled mentally ill and what we label as good and bad. My colleague was an articulate, insightful young man who was not running around with an axe and chopping up people—and there was no evidence that would ever happen. He knew he was exploring a different reality. He knew he didn't want to take the medication, and he knew he could explore a different reality without medical intervention.

Of course there are people with such extreme behavioral issues that a society may need to intervene. The level of intervention is still being debated. While we're trying to sort that out, it's helpful to remember that each person is an individual following his or her own path. Even if society must restrict access of some people to the world for safety reasons, it could enrich our entire society immeasurably if we were to stop making assumptions about them and judging them—and more justly support them in finding their way.

I realize that my discussion of the psychological aspects of our journeys may not be popular with many people with FM, CFS, and MCS since so many of us have worked long and hard to convince the medical community that the conditions are due to physical factors rather than psychological ones. First of all, I want to make sure that my rejection of a label of mental illness for myself is not made at the expense of individuals who do have a diagnosis of a psychiatric disability. One is not better than the other. One is accurate, and the other is not; an accurate diagnosis gives us the tools to support our health more appropriately.

Many of us have questioned our own observations, experiences, and sanity when we were told our symptoms were imagined or caused by psychological problems. I feel I must have a discussion about psychological issues to make sense out of this part of the experience. The thing that helped me make sense out of this issue was connecting the dots between what has been labeled as psychological and what was emerging for me as spiritual. I no longer attempt to prove my sanity; I feel a growing consciousness and trust of Self.

In the first season of Showtime's award-winning *Homeland* series, Carrie Mathison has bipolar disorder. She ostensibly experiences a break with reality, is hospitalized, and undergoes electroshock therapy. When you dissect the story more carefully, it seems that what really happened was that everyone who Carrie trusted was telling her she was imagining things with the prisoner-of-war-turned-terrorist Nicholas Brody. Because she trusted them more than she trusted herself, there was only one conclusion she could draw. It wasn't because she had bipolar disorder that she got so confused and panicky; it was because she didn't trust herself.

Many people do this to themselves every day—whether or not they have a psychiatric or physical disability or a chronic illness. In my spiritual quest to find meaning and purpose in my illness, I recognized that the most profound and life-changing gift that it held for me was learning just how much I really can trust what I know, what I observe, what I experience, what I want, and where the source of my real power comes from. That shift in my view of reality caused a number of things in my life to change. Some of them were scary, but once I crossed that threshold, there was no going back. The last time a colleague asked if I knew that some people thought my disability was psychological (which wasn't long ago), I simply replied, "Yes, I know, but I don't care anymore. I just do what I have to do to take care of myself." Listening to my inner wisdom helps me remember how valid my own experience is.

Whenever I am at an event where the air quality is harmful to me, or I'm in too much pain or too fatigued to keep participating, I simply leave. I no longer worry about what others think or say about me. I value my health more than I value their opinions. That was a huge chasm for me to cross, especially growing up as someone who looked to others for validation. The chronic illness served as the mechanism that gave me the opportunity to cross that chasm. Once I understood that, the concept of purpose in all things began to come into focus.

I would never be willing to give back what I have gained— even if it meant having a life of total health.

CHAPTER 7

The Archetypal Journey

You healers look to keep a level eye here, and anything
that falls below that line, you call illness, disease,
sickness, or catastrophe. Yet we ask you to see whatever
falls below that line as opportunity instead. For the
art of mastery is taking something that has fallen
below that line and using it in its highest form.
—Steve Rother[14]

A s a voracious reader, one of the most enriching results of exploring the literature on healing and spirituality has been learning that I can adopt wholeheartedly, adapt, or reject any of it by testing it out in my own life. The concept of archetypes and their roles in supporting our journeys is one of those areas where I found help unexpectedly. Archetypal ideas, images, or patterns are defined in several different ways, but most of us think of them in terms of a type of person. If you hear that someone is a clown, you get an immediate sense of what that person may be like.

Caroline Myss describes many common archetypes in *Sacred Contracts: Awakening Your Divine Potential.* We're familiar with many of them, but we may not realize it until we read her work and ponder what qualities seem to drive us. Some of the formal archetypes that she identifies are Hero, Damsel in Distress, Martyr, Servant, Victim, and Femme Fatale.

One of the archetypes that Myss also discusses is the Wounded Healer, which shows up in people who have experienced physical injury, illness, or other hardships. Rather than the person's life journey being about healing the illness, it becomes a process of transformation. I identified with this archetype because of my experiences. I started out with the intent to get well, but then I realized what happened was a spiritual metamorphosis instead. I don't think we have to have the Wounded Healer archetype to find meaning and purpose in illness and disability though.

I have experienced chronic illness itself as archetypal. All cultures have definitions, social mores, religious philosophies, and public policies about chronic illnesses and disabilities that come from deeply held beliefs about their meaning and implications. There is a mythology around chronic illness and disability, and many of us accept it.

Movies use archetypal personalities to tell their stories—spurned lovers, runaway brides, abandoned children, dishonorable thieves, cold-blooded killers. We instantly get a sense of those people's journeys even before we hear the specifics of their stories.

Movies, books, and other media have provided venues for exploring various archetypal processes for people with disabilities and chronic illness: the poster child, Jerry's kids, Tiny Tim, the Hunchback of Notre Dame, the village idiot, the madwoman locked in the attic (Mr. Rochester's wife in *Jane Eyre*), the town drunk, the embittered blind man, the miserly invalid (Mr. Potter in *It's a Wonderful Life* was played by Lionel Barrymore who was actually disabled at the time so the wheelchair was not a prop, but the mean-spirited symbolism was still there), the sexless paralyzed person, the oversexed drug addict, and the evil maimed person (Captain Hook). It is not unusual for the villain in a story to have a physical or mental difference. In recent years, there have been a growing number of more positive (and ordinary) character roles for people with disabilities in movies and television programs.

The person with chronic illness is often portrayed as a hypochondriac who annoys everyone with complaints and neediness. Some consider us a drag to be around and don't take us seriously. One of my favorite movies is *Sleepless in Seattle* since I am a romantic at heart (now there's a fun archetype for many people). In the beginning of the movie, Meg Ryan's character has a boyfriend who has allergies and sleeps with a room humidifier to help his breathing. He also has an allergy to wheat. There were subtle and not-so-subtle clues that Meg Ryan's character was displeased with his imperfections. It wasn't surprising that she chose the handsome, healthy Tom Hanks character over her sickly boyfriend. That's the way many think about the desirability of a love interest. The person must be vigorous and healthy.

Having an illness that is considered psychological or not real is another subset of the archetypal journey. The theme of not being believed and then not trusting yourself (Carrie Mathison's journey in *Homeland*) is expressed in untold numbers of movies and television programs. The person who witnesses a murder and finds the body is missing when he brings the police back to the scene is a popular story. Romantic partners who won't accept that you're not cheating on them and the person wrongly imprisoned for a crime he didn't commit also show up a great deal. To me, these stories aren't about murder, jealousy, or an imperfect judicial system. They are about the journey of a character-who-is-not-believed finding inner truth and a voice.

One of the most profound archetypal journeys we work with in the independent living movement is among people with disabilities who are institutionalized and want to get out and live in the community. Many times, they are prevented from doing so, not because of their medical condition, but because of bureaucratic red tape, the lack of affordable and accessible housing in the community, and professionals and family members who oppose their living in the community because of safety fears.

Helping someone get out of an institution is considered so fundamental to the concept of disability rights that a Supreme Court decision was handed down in 1999. *Olmstead vs. L. C.* declared that the unnecessary segregation of individuals with disabilities in institutions may constitute discrimination based on disability. Most centers for independent living have assisted people with disabilities in getting out of institutions as a matter of principle. Since 2014, with the reauthorization of the Rehabilitation Act, centers are required to provide this service. To most advocates in the independent living movement, institutionalization against one's will is akin to unlawful imprisonment.

Some colleagues and friends with psychiatric diagnoses tell me that the most disturbing aspect of being labeled with a mental illness is involuntary commitment to a treatment facility and being forcibly held down while medications with harmful side effects are injected. There are parallel movements to the disability rights and independent living movements started by mental patients who seek justice and the right to make one's own decisions and control one's own life.

The recovery movement, survivor movement, mad pride movement, and mental patients liberation movement brought about changes in mental health systems that treated individuals with psychiatric diagnoses as if they would never recover, would probably get worse, and must always be under the supervision of a psychiatric authority. Many people with psychiatric disabilities do in fact recover (some without intervention), and many of those who continue to have symptoms are teaching us that living effectively with a condition is workable once they have gained a sense of self-determination and personal empowerment.

Imprisonment in any form—whether in a medical facility, actual prison, or in ordinary life circumstances when we feel as if we are trapped and have no power—can provide a deeply transformative opportunity to discover the true meaning of freedom. Even in restrictive physical environments, our souls remain free to explore and create. In the situations of my life where I have felt imprisoned, I was willing to do anything to free myself of that feeling, regardless of the consequences. I would approach those situations differently now, with fewer struggles, fear, and panic, but I don't regret the choices I made. Once I experienced freedom of spirit, there was no going back.

Some of us are born to experience being taken care of. Some are born with the opportunity to be caregivers. Others are taking care of ourselves amidst the challenges and barriers inherent to living with physical or mental differences. Some people experience good health and well-being for a long time, and then they have significant changes to their mental or physical states. They may have never given their health a second thought until the changes happened—or they may have constantly worried about losing their health. Some people are born without the ability to feel pain. Some of us feel it more acutely than others. Some people decide to get pregnant with the expectation that their offspring will be completely healthy and whole, and then they experience a crisis of conscience when their babies are born with mental or physical differences. There is something in each of these journeys for the people who experience them.

Thinking about my own experience with chronic illness as a process wherein I could find my own wisdom opened up a vast world to me. Chronic illness may not be explicitly identified as an archetype, but it does have an archetypal quality that can aid us in understanding and negotiating our processes. Archetypes are thought to be tools and avenues that allow us to explore dimensions of the physical realm that we couldn't without the context they bring to our lives. They give us parameters to work within, but they don't define who we truly are. Every journey gives us the opportunity to find the divine within. Person-with-a-congenital-disability, person-with-an-acquired-disability, person-with-a-chronic-illness, person-with-a-life-threatening-illness, person-with-a-psychiatric condition, and person-institutionalized-against-his-will all bring certain qualities to a life journey. As spiritual beings in time and space and limits and boundaries, they offer us choices for the journey. We can observe them, work with them, learn from them, deny them, or view them as punishment or opportunity as we choose.

The mythologies of our societies are not likely to change quickly. Societies prefer to grow slowly and deliberately. I'm not saying that our stories should change. We get to decide for ourselves what our stories will be. We may or may not be able to change the physical, mental, and circumstantial characteristics of our lives at the present moment.

I discovered that I have real power in the midst of the circumstances of my life when I remember that I can always change my mind about what I think their *meaning* is. Unraveling the mythology that had defined the way I perceived my chronic illness gave me the information I needed to break out of that mythology and live the empowered life I was seeking. I learned that I could create a different adventure from the life of drama and tragedy that I used to experience.

CHAPTER 8

Or Is It Spirit, Spirit, and Spirit?

R am Dass, author of *Still Here: Embracing Aging, Changing, and Dying*, experienced a stroke that left him partially paralyzed. He now uses a wheelchair. He says in his book, "Because I'd spent my adult life concentrating on the realms of the spirit, I'd always been able to rationalize the distance I maintained from my body by saying that my detachment was a spiritual witnessing of the physical form. But that had been only partly true. The truth is that I distanced myself from my body. I saw my body as merely a vehicle for the soul. I ignored it as much as possible and tried to spiritualize it away."[15]

I deeply appreciate what Ram Dass shared about his journey because I had tried so hard to affirm away my illness. I had focused only on my spiritual journey until the realness of my health issues brought me back to earth. My illness became the driving force, and ultimately the answer, for what I was searching for. As many other authors have written, what I found was not a cure but my Self. The search did not bring me perfect health, but it did lead me to wholeness.

I grew up believing I had a soul, but it was a vague notion of something intangible that hung out in some indefinable place. It would be rewarded or punished when my physical body died. In many ways, it was something that had nothing to do with my day-to-day life. When I became enamored with the new age movement, it was more believable to me that souls live again and again so that they can perfect themselves. Even that belief carried the weight of karmic rewards and punishment, albeit stretched out over a longer period of time.

When I was introduced to the idea that nothing really needs to be perfected if I am a spiritual being immersed in a physical experience, I couldn't grasp it or accept it. It seemed blasphemous and dangerous. My understanding of my divinity had always been couched in euphemistic terms such as "created in the image of God," "divine spark," "my higher self," "a little lower than the angels." To my way of thinking, that still made me something that could be destroyed at any time at the bidding of an all-powerful separate being.

I now believe that all is divine. That means that the Divine is not a *him* but a *her, him, them, we, you, it, me.* That means we are all an extension of the Infinite. You may have heard the concept that God is everything that you are, but you are not everything that God is. There's no aspect of you that is not your soul, but there's more to you as a soul than there is to you as a finite human. The part that really excited me about this way of thinking was that I began to understand that as soul, I am taking care of my physical self. With that knowledge, I started to understand the concept of trust.

Before I came to that understanding, I was confused about what it meant to recognize that we are spiritual beings. I pursued esoteric metaphysical teachings with the expectation that I would be able to master things like astral projection, curing sick people, and curing myself. It's not that these things were necessarily beyond my reach, but I realized that they're not relevant for everyone's journey.

I wondered if we had misunderstood the teaching in the Christian New Testament where Jesus said that if we have enough faith, we will be able to do the same things he did. I wondered why all the Christians I knew were not duplicating his miracles. Not that I didn't see things going on that seemed rather miraculous, but the larger picture seemed to be that there was still a lot of illness—even among people I knew who had enormous faith.

One of my friends was exploring this concept at the same time I was. He declared to me one day at church that he would no longer get colds because he knew he could simply believe he would stay well and make it so. Knowing him as I did, I think he did believe that. Not only did he get more colds, he died a few years later from pancreatic cancer. He never said anything to me about changing his understanding of what faith means, but as I watched him go through the last few months of his life, I saw a man with a great deal more peace and acceptance than the man who boldly declared that he had gained power over illness a few years earlier.

When my own illness began to linger after what seemed like superhuman (and supernatural) efforts to get well, I began to realize that my spiritual quest had led me to striving to no longer be human. It was as if in recognizing that my true essence was Spirit—a boundless energy and force—I couldn't possibly want to continue being human. It was certainly true that I didn't want to continue being sick, but it encompassed more than that. Some part of me believed that being human was a bad thing. It was a test wherein I had to prove I was worthy. If I could live in a spiritual state, meditating, praying, affirming the reality I wanted, staying in the present moment, I would *be* the Spirit that I believed myself to be. I was so focused on my spiritual potential that I lost sight of my human potential.

I came to believe that the purpose of incarnation into physical form is about Spirit pretending to be finite for the purpose of exploring time and space, limits and boundaries. I started to think that it was ironic that some of us in flesh keep trying to disincarnate into spiritual formlessness so that we won't have time and space or limits and boundaries to deal with. Boundaries give us a challenging and fun way to be creative. If all were energy and no form, there would be no human game. It is not bad to have restrictions, even if they're painful, and we don't have to transcend all the restrictions to prove anything. Our purpose is to explore them, see the nuances and shades of distinction between them, notice how we feel, what we prefer, and decide to what degree we are able to change or accept what is.

Maybe some souls are exploring how to create anything and everything their finite selves want, but I realized I was interested in exploring the *meaning* of creation. Probably because of my professional life, I came to see that disabilities and chronic illnesses are opportunities to redefine what we mean by creativity. In accepting this premise, issues of mechanical adaptations, assistive technology, and physical, mental, and emotional accommodations for people with disability and chronic illness took on a much larger dimension. Medical science hasn't yet grown new limbs for amputees, but rehabilitation engineering has certainly designed amazing prostheses. If the goal of people with leg amputations is to be able to walk and run again, they are likely to find a mechanism to do that now. On the other hand, if their goal is to grow new limbs, their journey may be about the odyssey of unanswered questions instead. (However, the advances in science are happening so quickly that nobody knows what we'll see in our lifetimes.)

In the earlier days of physical rehabilitation, people with physical disabilities were generally pushed to do everything they possibly could—regardless of how inefficient or time-consuming the activities were. The belief was that the person had to be returned to as much "normalcy" as possible—whatever the physical, emotional, or financial cost. People who had polio were often required to walk with crutches to keep them upright. To use a wheelchair meant you were an invalid. The wear and tear on some people's shoulders and backs from walking with crutches added another layer of disability for some. It was not unusual to be told to "go home and practice" if someone couldn't manage a physical activity. The inference was that the person should be able to do every task of daily living to some degree.

Many of today's consumers with disabilities (if they have resources) are given more choice in how they manage their activities. Individuals who are able to walk with crutches can decide if they want to spend several minutes walking across a room or use a wheelchair so they can get there more quickly. Accessibility design in homes and buildings allows more options. Changes in building codes and civil rights legislation for people with disabilities have created ways to push the boundaries. There are, no doubt, a lot of people who were required to tie their own shoes, regardless of how long it took them, who were relieved by the introduction of Velcro.

One of the things that amuse many of us in the independent living movement is that some of the people who opposed passage of the Americans with Disabilities Act as being too expensive and unnecessary are getting older and discovering that their bodies are no longer functioning as they did before. Ironically, they are benefitting from access design in buildings, transportation systems, and adaptive technology. Baby boomers will play a growing role in raising consciousness about disability and environmental and attitudinal barriers— naturally and without even realizing what they're doing. Small business owners will think less about the cost of modifications to their buildings and more about the lost revenue if a growing number of their potential customers can't get into and function in their stores.

Most people who have physical and mental changes as the result of aging don't think of themselves as acquiring a disability. They think of themselves as getting older and deteriorating. This absence of being labeled as someone with a disability is helping make accommodations and adaptations more socially accepted. Just as curb cuts proved to be beneficial for parents pushing baby strollers as well as wheelchair users, many of the enhancements in our environments and technology are normalizing the differences in the way we all function. We're acknowledging that every person on the planet has his or her own way of being in the world. We can make the world inclusive of everybody if we make the time and commitment to think about how we construct and manage it. We don't have to put labels on people to accomplish this.

Moving from the belief that I could and should create anything that I wanted to the belief that I can explore creation within limits and boundaries doesn't mean that I can't keep pushing those boundaries, experimenting, and setting new goals. It simply means seeing reality for what it is, so that I can live, love, participate, eat, play, sing, and dance in whatever way works for me—for now. I can keep wishing for something different. I can plan, experiment, and implement. I can dream as big as I want to. But if I do these things from "you are here" on the map of my life, I bring a great deal more power and force to it. Being grounded in a perspective that I am a spiritual being immersed in a physical experience with limits and boundaries brought an end to bemoaning my circumstances. It enabled me to get back to the business of living. This perspective also enabled me to end the belief that I am a victim in all the ways I was carrying that energy.

CHAPTER 9

A Framework for Change

When I was a teenager and young adult, the world was exploding with revolution and breaking down old systems and structures that were no longer serving us. Growing up in Jackson, Mississippi, I witnessed some of the most volatile events that the world experienced in those days. I worked one summer at the Woolworth where sit-ins took place at the soda fountain. I walked by the buses with "Freedom Riders" emblazoned across the sides. Medgar Evers was murdered days after I graduated from high school, and I witnessed Byron De La Beckwith being brought into the Hinds County Sheriff's Office in handcuffs (for his first arrest) the summer when I worked there.

I had the privilege of being one of five students at my college who greeted Robert Kennedy when he arrived on campus while visiting Jackson during the civil rights hearings. After the passage of the Civil Rights Act of 1964, some Jackson restaurants started calling themselves private clubs, and patrons had to knock on their locked doors. If you were the right color, you were allowed in.

My college started to voluntarily enroll black students, accepting six African Americans the year I was a senior. I worked on the college switchboard, and I was on the receiving end of an angry caller who withdrew her financial support because of the change in policy. I accepted a ride from a black classmate and her mother for an off-campus activity, and I realized as we were driving down Capitol Street that I could have been killed for riding in a car with two black people. There was an air of defiance and fear that permeated Jackson.

When I moved to Detroit, my education about changing paradigms really began. I worked in the inner city at a large vocational rehabilitation facility, beginning shortly after the riots of 1967. Blocks around our agency were burned out and boarded up. I had gone from negotiating my way through the white supremacist culture of my childhood to being in the minority in a heartbeat. As open-minded and progressive as I thought I was, I became deeply challenged by working with African Americans and people with disabilities who were equals or superiors rather than second-class citizens. I was surrounded by people who looked different from me. The conditioning of my childhood surfaced, and I began to understand how unconscious and ingrained my prejudices were. I still had a lot of work to do.

Since the sixties, the world has undergone radical changes in cultural sensibilities. One thing that is changing rapidly is that people of all characteristics are being accepted and included as beings of the same worth as every other person. There is a growing awareness of the intersection between race, ethnicity, age, gender expression, sexual orientation, religious practice, and physical, mental, and emotional ability. If someone is marginalized because of who they are, it reinforces the perception that we are all less than we are. Our growing commitment to increased human rights is an outward sign of our growing consciousness about our true Selves. No individual or group of people is outside the bounds of sacredness.

Human rights as a political and social construct have both personal and planetary meanings. The search for them is another one of those mechanisms that souls use for exploring the concepts of power and empowerment. The quest for human rights within the cultural and social structures of the physical world is only one of many paths to empowerment. There are so many possibilities for finding and becoming ourselves that we can't list them or even know them all.

In the independent living movement, we talk a lot about the concept of empowerment for people with disabilities. One of the stated goals of peer-driven independent living services is to assist individuals to become self-advocates, to find their own voices, and to make choices based on what they prefer rather than what a parent, an institution, or a professional is telling them they should want. It's a long, arduous process for some people with disabilities, particularly if they've lived in an institution for a long time or been sheltered at home by their parents. If the only choice you've ever been given is whether to put on the green shirt or the red shirt in the morning, it's difficult to gain a sense of identity or develop basic skills in making decisions and managing the details of your life.

Although we use the term *empowerment* frequently, we talk around it in the independent living field because it's not culturally acceptable in publicly funded human service organizations to talk about empowerment as the soul-level concept that it really is. We know it's something pretty intangible, but we tend to stick with more psychological definitions (self-actualization, enablement) to be safe. Many view power as something that comes from civil rights, laws, and justice. These are some of the outcomes we seek in the independent living field. It seems to be a necessary and natural step in the process toward finding and claiming our authentic power—the power that transcends what anyone or any system gives us.

The concept of empowerment originated in the seventeenth century in the legal realm to convey the process of investing authority or authorizing someone to do something. It was later picked up by the civil rights and women's movements as a way of expressing increased social and political power. These are important definitions that we need to keep in our social structure. But they don't and can't reflect the process of empowerment that is available to us when we recognize that our real power is something that comes from within ourselves, not from without. The legal definition is about someone else bestowing authority upon us. The political definition is about the passage of laws, the implementation of policies, and changing social structures that give us more control over our destinies. These definitions suggest that power is something that must be taken and guarded because there's never enough to go around.

As a direct result of the disability rights movement, medical, rehabilitation, and mental health systems have been gradually treating us less as case numbers and more as self-determined adults—not just because we have wrenched new behaviors out of such systems through political action and policy changes forged in the heat of revolution; but because, more fundamentally, we alter the way we view ourselves. That alteration becomes the tool for transformation.

The disability rights movement was founded by numerous individuals with disabilities around the country when they realized they were considered problems by society because they had physical or mental differences. Just like people of color, individuals with different sexual orientations, women, and seniors have been recognizing that they aren't defective or inferior just because someone declared that they are. People with disabilities figured out they could change how society treats them if they changed their own minds about what it meant to have a disability. They became educators who enlightened the rest of us that the real problem was that professional, institutional, and parental control over people, the inaccessible environment, and cultural attitudes were barriers to inclusion. If we could fix the barriers, having a disability was much less problematic.

The disability rights movement has not yet had the same level of attention from the media and mainstream public as the women's, civil rights, and LGBT (lesbian, gay, bisexual, transgender) movements have. The concept of ableism (discrimination in favor of able-bodied persons) is not as commonly known as racism, sexism, homophobia, and ageism. People with disabilities have taken the concepts of segregation and separate but not equal to a whole new level of discussion that the larger society is just beginning to understand. I think it's because people with disabilities have historically been viewed as charity cases who were to be pitied and taken care of—a designation that was not given to other groups. There's a condescension that many people with disabilities feel from others that would not be tolerated by people in other minority groups.

When the media does a story on someone with a disability, it's frequently about how brave and courageous the person is and how he or she overcame the disability. The word *overcome* is not generally used in the same way that it's been used in the civil rights movement to indicate people subjected to racism will someday be accepted and integrated into society. Instead, when used with people with disabilities, it generally means that they will get over or rise above the disability. Many people with disabilities have commented that the concept of overcoming a disability in this context suggests that they are not okay as they are. They must somehow change or achieve something impressive to be acceptable. People with disabilities don't yet enjoy the same sense of political correctness that other groups have acquired.

If you're a mountain climber who is blind, a skier with paralysis, a genius with autism, or a celebrity with bipolar disorder, you will blow their socks off. If you're an ordinary person—raising a family, working, shopping at the grocery store, and managing the complexities of a disability—there won't be much interest from the world. Many in the disability rights arena believe that's because physical, intellectual, and behavioral differences are still considered pathology rather than ordinary life experience.

We seldom hear about the civil rights of people with disabilities outside of the disability rights community. The connection between disability rights and civil rights still seems fuzzy in the minds of the media and the general public. The prejudices toward people with disabilities have been subtler and are often embedded in the care they are given. It's considered uncharitable in our culture to have negative feelings toward people with disabilities (unless they have been labeled as having a mental illness—then it's often considered an appropriate reaction). Many people with disabilities experience discrimination that manifests as protective benevolence. Nondisabled people often behave as if they believe it is their duty to take care of the person's body, mind, and soul, and not think in terms of equality and human rights. The more significant the disability is—and the more the person with the disability is dependent upon other people for physical or cognitive assistance—the more easily this dynamic can happen.

It also happens to those of us with invisible chronic illnesses. People who love us—or even people who don't know us well— sometimes want to jump in and manage us. They may become afraid for us and think we're not handling things properly. Sometimes there's an air of superiority when the other person tells us they know what treatments and life choices we should be making. The unspoken message is that we are incompetent because we haven't made the choices they think are right. One of the lessons some of us with disabilities and chronic illnesses are exploring is how to maintain boundaries without rejecting the person who wants to take care of us.

The notion of discrimination toward people with disabilities did not come into play until people with disabilities started to say, "I want to leave this institution (or my parents' home and care), go to school, get married, and get a job!" Society finally began to examine how the built environment, social policies, and attitudes were preventing them from doing those things. Some of the slogans that emerged in the disability rights movement were: "You gave us your dimes, now give us our rights" and "Choices not charity." The disability rights and independent living movements have demonstrated how it is possible for many people with significant and profound disabilities to be self-determining and stay in control of their own destinies while still utilizing the physical, cognitive, or emotional supports that other people can provide. There is a growing understanding that independence for any human being entails interdependence because most of us function better in a community. However, collaboration and cooperation do not require giving away our personal power and self-determination.

For a group of people of any characteristic to start redefining how they are characterized, they have to arrive at a certain degree of consciousness and self-awareness. That's when real empowerment starts happening. When I felt powerless, I didn't know how to find that power within myself. It seemed like something external that I had to search for—or somehow have it bestowed upon me. People told me to embrace it or claim it, but I didn't know where to find it. I didn't know where it was closeted until I could claim it. I hadn't yet hit upon the steps to take to embrace it. When I experienced authentic power emerging from within me, I realized it had been there all along. It shifted my perception about what real power is and made it come into focus.

People with disabilities have gained enough political power to demand and claim their rights. As a result, other people are beginning to treat them differently. Society is beginning to change, and arenas that were previously denied people with disabilities are opening up, including voting, owning property, employment, housing, education, and marriage. People with all sorts of differences are gaining an equal place at the table and continuing to grow in how they define themselves. The opportunity now is to realize that power was internal all along. I came to understand that power was mine because I *am* power—not political, social, or cultural, but soul power with a purpose and a path.

Being labeled as a hypochondriac and someone who was imagining my illness was a more significant part of my journey toward empowerment than the illness itself. It was the sense of shame that I carried, that I must be a loser if I'm defined in that way, that propelled me toward finding my truth. I decided to re-define the problem. Who I am, what genes I was born with, the personality I have, and the level of physical, mental, and emotional capacities that I live with are not wrong. I am who I am. I grow and I change, but that's a process. And if I believe my being here and experiencing what I'm experiencing has relevance, then I must reject the opinion of anyone else who thinks they know what's right and wrong about me. The experience of being challenged about the validity of my illness has sharpened my intuition, self-trust, self-acceptance, self-esteem, and self-respect. What I viewed as one of my greatest weaknesses turned out to be one of my greatest assets.

No one else has the authority to declare that my experience with chronic illness is real or not real, psychological or physiological, a dream, a tragedy, or anything else. They may have a right to speak their minds in a nation of free speech, but I—in partnership with my soul—am the only person who has the authority over my own life. Now that I know that, I am able to forgive anyone who thought otherwise, including myself.

It's natural to become angry when we first recognize that what we believed about something is built on a partial lie. But what we're learning is that the entire human construct was designed around partial truths; and our ability to see each other more clearly, for the brilliant beings we all are, is growing. Our secret hatreds and fears and sense of separation are becoming transparent so quickly through our networked world with its instant communication that we're able to move almost as one entity toward smoothing out the kinks. We have lower tolerance for discrimination, prejudice, and self-hatred—not because we reject people who harbor those things but because we're interested in truth.

Our world seems to be in chaos at the moment, but looking with a higher view, we might see the new world that is emerging. Everyone has something to say. How interesting to stop and listen.

CHAPTER 10

The Power of Acceptance

I have no idea what I'm supposed to do.
I only know what I can do.
—Capt. James T. Kirk, *Star Trek: Into Darkness*[16]

The Little Engine That Could is a huge metaphor in our culture for children and adults alike. The story brings an amazing transformative energy for the individual who feels inadequate. It has been an effective resource for many of us who struggled with feelings of inferiority. Teachers, parents, and friends may have adopted the spirit of the story and told us to never use the word *can't*. We may have been encouraged to say, "I can do anything," and "all things are possible." I have deep appreciation for the gift this kind of thinking brought on many levels. I believe it has also been a gift of universal relevance.

However, for those of us with chronic illness and disability, the word *can't* became such a no-no in our culture that many of us became afraid to use it. It wasn't politically correct. It's certainly a no-no within the realm of creating your own reality thinking. "There is nothing we can't accomplish." We hear that almost daily in news reports and feature stories about people who have accomplished amazing feats.

I saw a story on the national news about a child with a disability that reflects some of this thinking. A young boy with a profound congenital hearing loss had undergone cochlear implants, electronic devices that provide a sense of sound. Before the surgery, his mother wasn't optimistic about his future, but with the enhanced hearing, she thought he would be able to do anything or be anything. First of all, it's possible that her son could have accomplished anything he chose to do *with* a profound hearing loss (think of Marlee Matlin). It is also possible that with enhanced hearing he will still encounter failures and not achieve everything he hopes to. Expecting a certain outcome in either direction may not result in what she believes will happen. We may assume our lives will be better if we are cured of an illness or disability. Maybe. Maybe not. It's possible that even more difficult challenges could show up.

Our intellect tells us it's not really true that we can do everything, but it's a game we've chosen to play because it's fun to talk about ourselves in that way. I was so invested in proving my spiritual prowess that I refused to use the word *can't* until the limits of my abilities hit me over the head. When you literally collapse from exhaustion, you intimately understand the meaning of the word *can't*. When you're driving your car and can't remember how to get home from the office—a route you've driven hundreds of times—you know what *can't* focus means. When you start to move your legs to walk across a room and they give out, you get what *can't* walk safely today means.

The football players and military personnel who were portrayed as indestructible because of their rigorous training and well-honed athletic abilities but experienced head injuries are emerging into our collective consciousness as not being invincible. Brain injuries started receiving attention in the rehabilitation field in the nineties, but they have largely been out of sight and out of mind for the general public (like other invisible disabilities). Our television and movie action heroes are knocked unconscious over and over again, but they never experience any lasting damage. Why shouldn't our real-life heroes be unscathed?

We have had a similar history with posttraumatic stress disorder (PTSD) beginning with the "shell shock" of World War I, which later became "battle fatigue" and then PTSD. After Iraq and Afghanistan, combat veterans with PTSD were studied and more substantive data collected. Over the many years I have worked in the disability arena, I have known people with PTSD whose conditions were labeled a "moral failing," a "psychological problem," and a "neurological issue." For eons, people have focused more on the glory and valor of war than the impact on humans and the planet. Some of us are now reframing our definitions of PTSD and battle.

People who have acquired head injuries or PTSD are not defective or broken, but they now have opportunities to explore reality in different ways. And therein lies the adventure.

Many of us have come to have a new appreciation for the word *can't*. It's a useful word many times, but that doesn't mean we should use it carelessly. There are still many things that we're afraid we can't accomplish and don't allow ourselves to try. But consciousness gives us the freedom to explore the difference and stop being apologetic about the things we really can't do. We can do many things within limits and boundaries, but we can't do everything.

Even the indomitable James T. Kirk, captain of the starship *Enterprise*, had a sense of his limitations. In the situation quoted at the beginning of this chapter, he told Mr. Spock that he had no idea what he was *supposed* to do; he only knew what he *could* do. He was saying that he knew it was not useful to analyze all of the possibilities when he only had a few seconds to respond to the emergency. It was far more effective to act on what he knew his resources and ship's capabilities were. We don't need to keep trying to prove a point about how we have overcome our disabilities. It doesn't disempower us to acknowledge that we can't do something physically, mentally, or emotionally at the present moment. It disempowers us to keep proclaiming that we can accomplish anything, at any price, at any time.

When I lived in a city that was in the direct path of a hurricane, my neighborhood was not under mandatory evacuation, but I decided to evacuate anyway. I knew that the complexities of dealing with a disabling condition could be compounded by a lengthy power outage, damage to my residence, and a city in chaos. I suspected there would be gridlock on the main evacuation routes, and I left a day earlier than was recommended. I knew that if I were to run out of gas in the oppressive heat, with diesel and gasoline fumes hanging heavy in the air, I could be in serious trouble. It served me well to leave when I did. Many of those who left on the recommended day ran out of gas from the lengthy idling time. I understood my vulnerabilities and was fearful of potential harm to myself. I learned some important skills during that event that have continued to serve me well, but the most important lesson I learned was that I didn't need to be afraid. I was using my inner wisdom and the strategies I knew I had at my disposal. I knew what I *could* do. Moving beyond fearfulness to live one's life with trust and peace is a process that will be affected by many things, including the degree of trauma one has experienced and the neurological wiring that one is born with.

One of the opportunities for us in this discussion about *can* and *can't* is to examine our beliefs about the realness of limitations and what we expect that people should be able to feel and do. It's another opportunity to notice how harshly we sometimes judge ourselves and each other.

Defining my health condition as a disability (rather than an illness) was another significant key to unlocking the puzzle of how to make my life work. When I was still trying to find my way through the confusion, each time I called it an illness, I felt an expectation rise within me that I should get well at some point. With each treatment that led nowhere, the scab over my despair would be ripped off—and I would start to bleed again.

I am not suggesting here that others with FM, CFS, MCS, or any chronic condition should consider themselves disabled. Labeling anything is sometimes useful and sometimes not, depending on your personal goals. For me, this was one label that turned out to be useful because it reminded me of the tools I already had at my disposal through my profession. Working in the disability field for as long as I had, it might seem obvious that I would be drawn to a disability descriptor, but it wasn't obvious to me. I stammered over trying to explain my symptoms and limitations to others, and I often just went silent because of the experience of not being understood or believed. Fear of being judged fed my powerlessness.

Not long after I began working with my current employer, I felt panicky over not being able to focus and remember things. I was considering resigning and entering the ranks of poverty again. Most of my work might be characterized as intellectual in nature; it involves thinking, planning, discussing, facilitating group process, writing, and editing. A large part of the job is participating in or facilitating conference calls. On these calls, I would often have difficulty tracking the conversations. I would get confused about what had been said and who said it, and I would be hesitant to contribute to the discussion for fear I would say something off track. I couldn't hold a thought in my brain for more than a few seconds.

I had resigned from one position years earlier because of the cognitive difficulties and had struggled in other positions. I believed I was about to fail again. We were working with a national expert in adaptive technology at the time. Adaptive technology of the high-tech (computers, screen readers) and low-tech (canes, walkers, reachers, and grabbers) varieties was not new to me. And working with people with cognitive disabilities was certainly not new either. I had managed a program for people with traumatic brain injuries, and one of the things we assisted with was adaptive ways of remembering things: calendars with timers, pillboxes organized by days of the week, notebooks, sticky notes, and assorted other strategies. I hadn't learned much for myself. I thought I believed and understood the philosophy of taking care of myself, but I didn't yet understand how to translate that philosophy into personal practice.

It may seem odd to others that I couldn't connect the dots. After all, one of the ways that the independent living movement describes people with disabilities is *differently abled*. But within the context of thinking of myself as a person with an illness that was going to be cured at any moment (because I was supposed to be creating a different reality) and as someone who had been told her problem was psychological, it had just never seemed relevant. However, there was something about the work of the national expert on adaptive technology and my readiness to think about my life differently that led me to ask for a personal consultation with her. I didn't learn a great deal that was new from her because I had already learned a great deal in my professional role.

I finally allowed myself to think about my own needs. She was *my* mentor and guide. I finally saw that there was no difference between adaptations and accommodations if you have a chronic illness versus if you have been labeled as someone with a disability. The nature of the accommodations varies from person to person, but the process of making accommodations can offer benefits regardless of the particulars. Creating reality is by definition being creative. Creatively designing your environment, schedule, and activities is creating reality. A cure is not the only reality that has validity.

That experience set in motion a more systematic way of examining tasks, environments, limitations, strengths, and needs than I had ever undertaken before. I had previously approached the idea so haphazardly that much of what I had tried was incomplete and ineffective. Finding cleaning products and personal-care products that I could tolerate in my home, working at home, having air purifiers around me, asking others to refrain from using fragrances, resting before I was wiped out, affixing sticky notes all over my house (and hooray for cell phones with navigators, calendars, and timers), asking for help on conference calls, delegating responsibilities, and myriad other things became a way of life rather than an afterthought. I gave priority to meal planning, strategic scheduling of shopping, eating before I become too hypoglycemic to remember to eat, careful scrutiny of travel arrangements and hotel accommodations, faithfully maintaining my boundaries, and not compromising on things that have the potential to harm me. Taking care of the basics before I take care of anything or anybody else became a policy: *This is the way I live. This is the way I manage my life, my health, my job, and my energy.*

Accepting reality is at its most basic coming into alignment with what works. Having a disability or chronic illness, at the most fundamental level, means that one accesses the world in a different way. The person with a spinal cord injury who believes he will walk again and wants to pursue the emerging technology that is showing promise by recreating walking motions may conclude it's too impractical on a day-to-day basis and come to understand how liberating, rather than confining, his wheelchair is. But his exploration is not a failure. It may be the most useful process that person's soul knew to help him come to a deeper understanding of his new reality—and his role as a creator within limits and boundaries.

If one uses a wheelchair for mobility, building a ramp to get into one's home is more practical than having another person lift you and your wheelchair up and down the stairs, risking back injury and causing exhaustion. Working at home and having control over my environment and schedule liberated me and provided me with freedom from more severe exhaustion and debilitation.

I am mindful of how fortunate I am to work in a profession and for an employer that is committed to making accommodations for people with disabilities. Many people with chronic illnesses that affect their ability to work usually have two choices: either work in an environment that aggravates rather than supports their health or not work at all.

The choices we have before us at any given point are simply part of the journey. What is more useful than regretting what we don't have? Look at what we have in front of us and expend our energies creatively designing ways to maximize whatever it is. We can take another look and decide what we *can* do.

CHAPTER 11

Try Another Way

G oing through the experience of assessing everything in my life in terms of potential adaptations and accommodations taught me a new way of thinking about reality. I have a new strategy now. When I think I know what's going on, I turn my perception on its head to see if there's another explanation or another solution that makes sense to me.

Before I got involved in the independent living movement, I worked briefly as a diagnostic evaluator in an organization for people with intellectual and developmental disabilities. Many of the program participants were considered severely or profoundly disabled. One of the things we were asking them to do was disassemble and reassemble a carburetor to assess their skills in such things as spatial perception, manual dexterity, and problem solving. It was a difficult, often time-consuming challenge for some participants. Shortly after beginning the work, I was introduced to an approach developed by special education teacher Marc Gold called "Try Another Way."[17] Dr. Gold believed that even individuals with significant intellectual disabilities could learn if we altered the way we teach them.

This technique involved breaking a task down into its smallest components, giving physical cues (such as placing your hand on the participant's hand), giving the single verbal prompt, "Try another way," and using verbal praise at key points. The technique relied on the principle that if someone realizes there is another way to do something or think about something, he or she has the capability to approach it differently. It was certainly a different approach from typical behavioral strategies of the day, which involved repeatedly telling the person they were wrong.

Dr. Gold trained so-called unteachable people to assemble electronic circuit boards and bicycle brakes, many at competitive speeds. Almost 100 percent of the time, they learned quickly and efficiently.

As I implemented the technique in my evaluator role, I was amazed that I immediately experienced the same results. I didn't even have to hone my skills in using the technique because the technique was so powerful. The workers would immediately turn the parts they were attaching in different directions every time I said, "Try another way." And every single time, they would ultimately figure out how to put the carburetor back together.

Thinking differently about all sorts of things gives us options. I try to remember this when I start thinking that my life is impossible. For example, if I am thinking my fatigue or pain is preventing me from doing what I want to do today, I tell myself instead that the fatigue is a message from my body to rest. It's an opportunity—not a prison sentence.

There was a time when I would not have thought of asking for a ride in a cart or wheelchair at an airport. I didn't want to take up a spot that somebody else needed. Besides, I wasn't that disabled (or that old). But then I realized it was not necessary for me to arrive at my travel destination as wiped out as I usually was. I could do some things differently, and asking for a ride was an easy one.

I hadn't anticipated that taking such tangible, simple steps (accommodations and adaptations) meant that I had begun the process of accepting the disability and thus my life. It was acceptance of reality—not trying to create a different reality— that finally led me to ask for what I needed.

The accommodations I had previously asked for, such as working at home part of the time, were requested out of a feeling of desperation. I wanted money to get out of debt and a return to interesting work, but I knew I couldn't make it driving into an office every day. This new way of thinking about accommodations was coming from a different energy within me. *This is real, and I want to pay attention to it at a level that I've never done before.*

At times, I wanted to pretend I wasn't sick so I wouldn't be criticized by my family and my peers (and my own inner critic). I kept ignoring many of the things my body was telling me. At other times, I wanted to keep focusing on a cure and putting all my eggs into the cure basket. When I accepted the reality of the illness, my feelings of being punished by God and judged by others evaporated. It was simple. It was mechanical. And it worked.

This place of understanding was one of the biggest surprises of my journey since I had started the process of healing from the belief that the only goal that had merit was being cured. The view of reality we have created with movies and television programs is that we should never accept things as they are, and we should keep striving to find the pot of gold at the end of the rainbow. The doctor who gives us a negative prognosis is wrong, and we can prove it. We can find the miracle drug, endure any treatment, and always have enough money to pay for whatever needs to be done, including flying all over the world to find the answer. There's always a cure in a screenplay that's written that way.

Some people may find perfect health, but I found something else that turned out to be more precious to me: I found freedom. Freedom means being who I was born to be, exploring life on my own terms, and claiming my unique path.

Not everyone's journey is the same. It has taken a great deal of pressure off of me to remember that. One spiritual teacher said he didn't follow up with the doctor on his life-threatening illness after he had a healing experience because he knew he had been healed. Consulting the doctor would have given the disease power. He believed he had been cured, and he chose to walk in that belief. Historically, I would have taken that to mean that I also should have been healed by my faith. But these days, I accept that his journey may have been about something different than mine. His journey may have been about having faith in a cure. Mine has been about accepting the way things are *for now*—and accepting the disability and its limitations so my soul could explore the boundaries of those limitations.

Just because that person's journey may have been about a relationship between belief and a cure doesn't mean that everyone's journey in the physical realm should be the same. Some souls are exploring what patience or endurance looks like when they have a chronic or life-threatening illness. Some are focused on the effects of illness on a relationship. Others may be examining what frustration in the face of adversity feels like. Someone else may explore reality through traveling around the world or growing up in poverty or being Chinese. The list of possible experiences is as diverse as the souls who populate the earth.

Many of us want to believe our journeys ought to be the same as everyone else's journeys. There is a deeply entrenched conviction that if something is true for one person, it should be true for everyone. The stampede to follow the latest fad diet because one person claims to have lost a lot of weight with it is a good example of how we keep doing this. We will not be free of the diet machine until we adopt a policy of tuning into our own inner guidance and making choices based on what's relevant for us personally. The spiritual teachers whose books I've read are shining a light so I can see in the dark, but our experiences are not the same. What our souls are exploring is not the same.

The other belief of mine that was challenged as I sorted through what accepting reality means was my assumption that acceptance was the same thing as having a sense of futility. Those two things are quite different. The former expanded my world, and the latter created despair. Acceptance meant focusing on what was working—or what could work if I refocused my attention. Futility meant running the tape in my mind of all the ways that my life didn't work.

It was only through having the experience of my illness that I was able to clarify the difference between those two states. I'm not sure I would have explored it in the depth that I did without my illness. The reason the difference was useful to explore was because I had bought into the idea of never giving up that we see on posters and T-shirts. That kind of thinking is a benefit for some people who are exploring that dimension, but it exhausted me and kept me on a hamster wheel. I was trying to live up to some vague worldly standard, and I was dodging the truth that was staring me down.

Accepting reality also does not mean that we have to approve of the way things are and that we can't prefer things to be different. But preference is not the same thing as being invested in the outcome of what we prefer. To prefer simply means we like something better than we like something else. When we are invested in something, we move out of the present and into the future or the past. We say, "It should be different than it is. It shouldn't have happened the way it did." When we move out of the present, our power is diminished, which is another totally mechanical phenomenon.

I still use the term chronic illness when I refer to my health with most people because it's more understandable to them, but I now think of myself more in terms of function than of diagnosis. I learned this from my colleagues with more traditional disabilities. Shifting the focus changes the questions I ask myself. Rather than pursuing how I can convince someone else that I have an illness, I ask myself questions: What can I do today to manage my energy and keep my cognitive faculties steady? What safe, nonallergenic foods can I bring on a trip to manage my blood sugar?

How do we accept limitations without thinking like a "handicapped" person or staying focused on what we can't do?

How do we accept bodily changes as we age without thinking like a decaying old person? These are useful questions. We accept the differences as real, for now, and support ourselves thoughtfully and respectfully in dealing with them. Part of that respect comes from not judging the changes and limitations as bad or criticizing ourselves for having them in our lives.

Chronic illness and physical or mental changes have the potential to shape the character of our days, regardless of the goals we want to achieve. Supporting our needs first—before we undertake any activity—gives more control to us than to the limitations we're dealing with. It takes the focus off of what seems deficient and places it on what works. A modification here and an adaptation there don't cure one's physical or mental condition. They lessen or remove barriers, reduce frustration, and make life work better. Paying attention to what works keeps us mindful of doing the things that will support the highest level of wellness possible within the limitations that are currently before us.

CHAPTER 12

Who Do You Think You Are?

How could anyone ever tell you, you were
anything less than beautiful, how could anyone
ever tell you, you were less than whole.
—from the song *How Could Anyone*, music
and lyrics by Libby Roderick[18]

L iving in a world that believes that anyone with a disability or chronic illness is inherently inferior because they aren't "normal," and at some level are probably incompetent, many of us have struggled intensely with self-esteem issues. The world has changed dramatically on that score during my lifetime, and it continues to change exponentially. There is evidence daily that attitudes are changing. People are becoming more accepting and less judgmental. I see the world as a more inclusive place these days.

There is, however, such a deep-seated belief in our collective consciousness that disability and chronic illness are bad, tragic, and abnormal, that low self-esteem is still part of the package that many people with disabilities and chronic conditions are negotiating. Because we typically assume our identities because of the ways other people react to us, we usually are unaware of how these beliefs shape us. If we don't experience enough feedback that we are adequate, we may decide we are inadequate.

The feeling of deficiency isn't limited to those with disabilities or illnesses. From the moment we get up until the moment we go to sleep, many of us question whether we ate properly, dressed correctly, are thin enough, paid enough attention to loved ones, performed competently on our jobs, bought the right present for a friend's birthday, or used the right words to make a point. We measure just about everything we do and are on a scale of deficiency—even as we move toward the level of proficiency that we prefer. The hierarchical way of thinking is deeply embedded in us. We're never good enough.

I wasn't identified as a person with a disability when I was a child, and I was never prevented from entering a building or getting a job as an adult because of attitudes about my physical appearance and physical or mental competencies. Most of my feelings of inadequacy related to my chronic illness were self-imposed since most people didn't even know I had a disability. Opinions that I was an emotionally damaged person when people did find out added fuel to the fire.

Like many people, I pursued self-esteem for many years. I think I first heard the term in college, probably in a psychology class where we were discussing Abraham Maslow's hierarchy of needs. I remember classes at church that talked about building self-esteem. Over the years, I read and struggled and wondered why self-esteem was so elusive—even when I systematically worked on improving it.

I thought I understood the concept well enough. It had to do with how I valued myself, whether I felt positively or negatively about myself, what I've accomplished, and what emotional state I was able to create. I had after all accomplished quite a few things in my life. How could I not like myself? But the negative thoughts about my adequacy hung around my life, catching me at being imperfect. A great deal of that negative thinking centered on my weird illness.

Whatever its origin, low self-esteem was a central feature of my persona. I said affirmations, underwent hypnotherapy, and reminded myself that God and many wonderful friends and family loved me. I excelled at many things, but I still felt so small, I often wished I could disappear.

A number of spiritual teachers have focused on self-esteem as a fundamental source of spiritual power. This makes sense to me because the essence of self-esteem is about recognizing our inherent worth. But I found another term that was more useful to me than self-esteem. It was a prerequisite to ultimately being able to anchor self-esteem into my energy system. That concept is self-acceptance. On the surface, it may seem that those two terms are the same thing. In fact, they are substantially different. Self-acceptance is a natural extension of accepting reality for what it is—for now—and it is a natural extension of staying in the present moment. It is not an effort to like myself or approve of myself (the definition of self-esteem that I had adopted), which seemed consistently out of reach.

I would feel proud of myself for my accomplishments one day, but the next day, I would feel like a failure. I noticed that what I would be stewing about was not the absence of self-esteem, but how badly I felt about myself for the absence of self-esteem. Because I viewed having self-esteem as good and not having self-esteem as bad, just as I had measured disability and chronic illness, there was no possible outcome except to feel badly about myself for not yet having perfected self-esteem. It was part of the same hierarchical thinking that I viewed the world through. All things were good or bad, right or wrong, and I should or shouldn't experience them.

Self-acceptance is simply accepting myself as a spiritual being immersed in a human experience with warts, neuroses, physical and mental limitations, and unresolved emotions that are a part of my experience today, including accepting that sometimes I feel badly about myself on a given day. Like self-esteem, self-acceptance is not a psychological process but a spiritual one. When you know who you are and who you're not, there's really nothing to not accept.

Some deaf colleagues have modeled authentic self-acceptance for me. The independent living movement has always been defined as cross-disability because it encompasses equal access and choices for all (rather than on diagnoses of individuals). People who are deaf and hard of hearing have always been considered partners in the movement, but many deaf people have chosen not to be involved with the centers for independent living because they do not view themselves as having a disability. They think of themselves as speaking a different language.

Many deaf people have refused cochlear implants because they don't believe there's anything wrong with being deaf. The people I have known who made this decision weren't in a psychological state of denial. They were simply accepting themselves as they are. The deaf boy in chapter 10 could identify more with Deaf culture as he grows up and decide to reject the implants. That could provide an interesting journey for him (and for his mother). However, it should not be misconstrued that those who choose to have cochlear implants don't accept themselves. I use this only as one example of how we make assumptions about what's good and bad or right and wrong in someone else's life. Each person is an individual with the right to choose.

You don't need to have a disability to become trapped in a maze of hierarchical thinking. Many of us automatically criticize ourselves for just about everything, including being overweight, having bad hair days, forgetting things, or experiencing negative emotions. We turn the so-called problem of losing our keys into feeling bad about ourselves for losing our keys. This forms a layer that creates a barrier to resolving the situation we're confronted with. With chronic illness and disability, it is useful to ask ourselves: "Is the problem my physical or mental condition, or is the problem that I'm criticizing myself for having the condition?"

Self-acceptance was a more useful goal for me than going after self-esteem because when I do slip back into feeling badly about myself, if I accept that I'm still in process with self-esteem, I can allow myself to have the feelings for now. I know they will pass. I may feel good about myself tomorrow and feel bad again the next day. There's an ebb and flow with self-acceptance because it recognizes the authentic human experience. Growing in self-acceptance—*getting off my case for being an imperfect human being*—has increased access to feeling good about myself. It is a more respectful way to treat myself. When I treat myself with more respect, a natural result is to like myself more.

One of the tools I have found to be especially effective for getting unstuck with self-condemnation is meridian tapping or emotional freedom techniques (EFT). Many techniques I have tried require more effort than I want to put forth. I'm always looking for energy-conserving ways to minimize fatigue.

Tapping has worked well for me in that regard, and it has proven to be successful many times. It has helped me deal with emotions that sometimes get tangled up with chronic illness and self-acceptance. I quickly find relief from self-criticism, frustration, anxiety, and anger. It can also be used to ease pain and other physical symptoms.

Tapping is based on the principle that negative emotions are caused by a disruption in the body's energy system. Tapping has been adopted by many psychologists, life coaches, and holistic practitioners. It is similar to acupuncture (without the needles) because it stimulates the body's energy meridians and opens energy flow. It also bypasses the mental gymnastics that we can get drawn into by trying to outsmart ourselves.

I'm not going to explain how to do tapping here except to mention that it involves tapping certain body points while saying certain phrases. Detailed explanations are available on the Internet at no cost.

The form of tapping I work with is an approach offered by Nick Ortner.[19] He expanded on the work of Jack Callahan and Gary Craig. It involves using a self-acceptance statement, such as, "I deeply and completely accept myself." Since self-acceptance was a goal of mine, this resonated well for me. Regardless of what the issue is or what emotion I'm feeling, I include the self-acceptance statement in the tapping process: *Even though I am embarrassed that I made a mistake in the project I'm working on, I deeply and completely accept myself. Even though I am frustrated that I'm in a lot of pain right now, I deeply and completely accept myself. Even though I'm feeling shame about my mental confusion right now, I deeply and completely accept myself.*

The approach acknowledges the layers of issues that I mentioned before. First is the so-called problem of feeling shame. The second is rejecting myself for feeling shame. After completing one or two rounds of tapping in a particular situation, I am almost always able to break the energy and move past the negative thoughts and feelings. Tapping has allowed me to move with increasingly greater ease through all sorts of emotional and neurological stresses.

Many of us are becoming more skillful at accepting ourselves these days, but it has been a challenge. We have more experience rejecting ourselves and focusing on what we believe has to be improved. Our worldview is that everything that exists must keep getting better. To accept ourselves as we are in this moment requires a 180-degree turn to look at the opposite of what we're used to seeing. It goes against the grain, but my experience with self-acceptance has been one of the most transformative energies I've ever experienced.

After working with self-acceptance for a while, I realized that I was easily negotiating my way through a set of stressful circumstances. It was not because of my on-the-spot powers of reasoning (which sometimes aren't there for people with certain types of medical conditions and disabilities). Instead, I created a framework for accepting myself, others, and challenging circumstances that kicked into gear and guided the transaction.

It's not easy to buck the tide of conventional wisdom that tells us there's something wrong with us because we have a chronic illness or disability, but the formula for doing so may be simple. When we accept things as they are—especially ourselves—we provide the fertile soil in which self-esteem and self-respect can grow. It is not the egotistical self-regard that the human world tries to avoid; it is a remembrance of our true wondrous Selves, having a human experience that's not good or bad, right or wrong, or should or shouldn't be happening.

CHAPTER 13

Be Here—for Now

Eventually, I realized … that my particular
sickness was far more effective training for
living in the moment than meditation.
—Anne Lipscomb[20]

It has been of interest to me that other people who have experienced serious chronic illness are writing about how the illness has revealed itself as a spiritual journey. Without having met these other authors, I feel kinship with them. Anne Lipscomb wrote *Poisoned by Pollution: An Unexpected Spiritual Journey*. She experienced a chemical injury at work and was involved in a claims process for many years to prove she was sick.

As if multiple chemical sensitivity wasn't challenging enough, Lipscomb jumped through exhausting legal hoops. After describing the process in vivid detail, Lipscomb says she began to recognize that her journey was about something more: a deeper relationship with her soul. She doesn't sugarcoat the illness; it still comes across as a pretty horrific experience. In spite of the pain and anguish—or perhaps because of it—she found something she had not expected. She learned to come into the present moment with a new wonder and appreciation for things she had hardly noticed before. The pain and other health issues forced her to pay attention, and they drew her into a deeper form of knowing and being.

Chills came over me as I read Lipscomb's words because she was articulating what I wanted to share in my own book. Part of my circuitous route with spiritual exploration had been trying to understand the concept of being in the *now*, which has been presented by numerous spiritual teachers. I attempted to develop a relationship with meditation on numerous occasions to accomplish that goal.

I grew up in a Christian tradition where prayer was thought of as a way of being. It was a mindfulness practice—rather than an activity that was done at specific times. The idea of trying to stay connected to God through the Holy Spirit was not new to me, but I didn't think about it as a connection to my own soul. The Sermon on the Mount found in the Christian New Testament has always been a favorite of mine. It's comforting and beautiful. Its poetic quality makes it easy to memorize and carry around in my heart. I knew the verse well that tells us, "Take, therefore, no thought for the morrow; for the morrow shall take thought for the things of itself. Sufficient unto the day shall be the evil thereof" (Matthew 6:34, KJV). I understood the word *evil* in this context means the challenges of daily life.

I tried not to worry about tomorrow. I tried to trust and believe all was well, but I felt anxious and panicky about how sick I was. I purchased a basic meditation book, believing it would teach me how to meditate, but I abandoned it after three attempts at reading it. I couldn't grasp what I was supposed to be experiencing when I meditated.

A few years later, I went to a meditation retreat at an ashram for a weekend. I hoped being in a sacred environment—among more experienced practitioners—would give me enlightenment by osmosis. It was a frustrating experience instead. I hadn't factored in my fatigue and how sharing a dorm room with several other people, getting up a couple of hours before my normal waking time, and sitting in a position that stressed my painful hip were going to affect my experience. As I understood it, I should have been able to rise above the uncomfortable physical dimension. It was another exercise where I felt as though I had failed.

I had a liberating conversation with a psychiatrist-turned-orthomolecular-physician about my difficulties in meditating. Orthomolecular medicine is an alternative health approach based on the principle that certain health issues can be treated by adjusting the imbalances or deficiencies of key chemicals in the brain through natural supplements such as amino acids, vitamins, and other micronutrients. He explained that someone with my health conditions was likely deficient in certain neurotransmitters, and that attempts to meditate might be as challenging as my attempts to focus. I was relieved by the possibility that there was a physical reason meditating was challenging for me (instead of a spiritual failing).

Many people have effective meditation practices, including people with chronic illnesses. I share my experience in case there are others with similar experiences who have judged themselves or judged meditation negatively because of it. For me, it was another one of those opportunities to remember that I am an individual and that measuring my experience against anyone else's is not useful.

Like many people, I also found the basic concept of staying in the present moment challenging. I used to live mostly in the past blaming myself and others for things that had happened to me or mistakes I had made. I was full of regrets and resentments. Then I moved into the future with wanting to create a different reality and getting invested in what I wanted, expecting things to turn out exactly as I envisioned them. Part of the soul journey is playing with the boundaries of time and space. If we are in the physical realm to explore the concept of time, it's not a failure when we can't stay in the present moment. We've all had much more practice in our exploration of the past or the future, and we are masters of that skill. Learning to be present in this moment is a process.

Human indoctrination taught us that the present moment is only a means to an end—without value in and of itself. We see its relevance and validity only in terms of what it will provide for the future. We like to revisit the past to determine what we will want in the future, and then we make choices in the present according to that. When we think or act based upon those things, there is no room for the present moment. Who and what is before us right now gets shut out.

Many of us understand the concept of living in the now. We try to practice it, but the discussion about staying in the present takes on a whole new dimension when you have chronic pain, severe fatigue, and other dysfunctions or debilitations. Some people say, "Just don't think about it," but they have probably never experienced a long-term serious illness.

When most things are affected by the symptoms, you may have to think about *now* in a different way. The spiritual discussions about forgiving the past and not worrying about the future may be realms that many human beings find relevant to explore, but when you have intense physical or mental symptoms, staying in the present moment becomes more mundane and basic. Every cell in your body may be screaming at you to escape from reality in search of relief.

Your mind may be constantly thinking about how soon you can lie down, get something to eat to bolster your flagging energy, or get away from whatever activity you're involved in. Conversations may be draining; you keep wishing they will end, but you feel obligated to be friendly and attentive. Staying in the present moment is a lovely thought, but if you don't know how to do it when the present moment feels awful, it's one more thing you can use to beat up on yourself because you haven't gotten it right.

Like Anne Lipscomb, my illness ultimately led me to understand and be able to practice being in the present moment. My goal ceased to be a successful meditation practice. Setting a goal of accepting my health condition opened the door to a mindful way of being in the world. I set out to discover how to survive the next ten minutes of trying to cope with the illness. The surprise was that getting through the next moments was only possible if I allowed things to be as they were instead of how I wanted them to be. I couldn't make useful choices about taking care of my needs if I was adamantly declaring that they shouldn't be the way they were.

Toni Bernhard eloquently described how to apply the concept of now to a serious illness in *How to Be Sick: A Buddhist-Inspired Guide for the Chronically Ill and Their Caregivers*. She shares her insights about this as a person with severe chronic fatigue syndrome who must spend the majority of her time in bed. Bernhard was a law professor who was well one day and sick the next, and she has never gotten well again. She had been a follower of Buddha's teachings and says the illness moved her into greater depth with her practice.

Bernhard uses phrases such as "woman on stool, brushing her teeth,"[21] to stay in the present moment and let go of stressful thoughts such as blaming herself for her illness. I liked this approach as soon as I read it because it instantly brought me back to what was actually happening in the moment. I decided to start using the idea for things that were overpowering my nervous system and raising my anxiety. I decided to add the phrase "for now" because of my tendency to think that something is going to be the way it is *forever* (i.e., sitting on stool forever). One of my phrases was: woman with nerve pain in neck *for now*.

Gradually something dawned on me. If there was any fear or anxiety lurking in my acceptance of things as they were— that I could be sick the rest of my life or get sicker tomorrow or develop another illness—I was not accepting the reality that was before me in the moment. I was making up a story about tomorrow and believing it was true. *I may get well tomorrow. I may not. I may be sick for the rest of my life. I may be sick for a short while.*

I realized it's okay if making up stories is where I am in my process right now. If I'm too overwhelmed, anxious, or exhausted to stay in the present moment today—or I'm too frustrated to accept my health as it is—I can use tapping, go take a nap, write in my journal, or go hug a tree to help break the energy. As I become more proficient with these kinds of tools, I notice that I more quickly remember that I am not the emotion I'm feeling. I am the observer of what I am feeling. The feeling becomes a curiosity.

This is what I'm feeling—for now. How interesting. This is what I know—for now. How thought provoking. This is what I'm capable of—for now. Ditto. If I'm thinking I can't afford a medical treatment I would like to try, I remember these are the resources I have at my disposal—for now. This is what's showing up—for now. If it's not working right now, leave it alone—for now.

I have years of experience living with the illness. My day-to-day symptoms, limitations, and capabilities are all over the map. I have collected an enormous amount of data in my brain on the possibilities. It is extremely easy to assume that I know what my future is going to be like. I have learned that all I really know is what the present moment looks like. I can guess about the possibilities for tomorrow based on the past. Accepting that I have limitations in this moment does not mean I have to believe I will always have these limitations.

By coming into the present moment, the possibilities and probabilities take on different meanings. My health condition provides an incentive to pay attention in a way that I wouldn't have without it. I move into an observer role without being disrespectful of the degree of difficulty of the thing I'm observing. I don't have to make guesses about the future. I can simply do what makes sense to me now. I can trust that whatever I need to know or do in this moment to prepare for tomorrow will be presented to me in this moment. What is in the moment is manageable without the burden of the past and the burden of the future.

If I want to run errands tomorrow, I can make a list of the priorities today, recognizing that I may or may not have enough energy to undertake all the activities. I star the things that are most important. If I wake up in the morning too sick to do any of them, I postpone things. If I have a business trip next month and want to get the most workable flight for me, I schedule it at least four weeks out, making my best guess about the workability of connections and layovers.

I've learned a lot about my body, and I get better all the time at making plans that support me. Some things don't work out, but I have strategies in my back pocket for those situations. I don't want to close doors for possibilities based upon who I was a year ago. If I stay in the present, that doesn't happen. When I stay in the present, I make more reasoned, self-supporting decisions—even if things don't work out as I project they will.

When I get to the outcome of the decision I made today and stay in the present, I will respond to unexpected circumstances in the present—with adult reasoning and the self-knowledge that is filed in my brain. I trust that the universe doesn't play gotcha with my so-called imperfections. Learning to trust is an unfolding process. If something seems negative on the surface, I can look at it in another way to see the opportunity.

How do we learn acceptance and presence? We practice, practice, practice. We can establish a ritual for making different choices. Just as we learned the ritual of rejecting ourselves, denying reality, and living in the past and the future, we can learn a new way of being. We can decide we want to live with greater consciousness and presence, and we can bring ourselves back to that intention when we remember to do so. We can cease punishing ourselves when we forget to do so. We don't have to sit in a lotus position to make progress. Each measure of pain, fatigue, mental confusion, irritable bowel episode, or asthma attack is an opportunity to be present, to be still, and to know.

Being present and being where I am at the moment is where I am. All the affirmations and dreams in the world are not going to change where I am at this moment. The next moment may be easier, but I won't know it until I get there.

CHAPTER 14

The Language of Power

We often lose track of the power of words because they are such an ordinary part of our daily lives. We sometimes use words that don't reflect what is true. It's not that we're liars (although some of us are at certain times), but the human game is based on illusion. Our language has the power to confuse our thinking. I experienced an eye-opening example of this a few months ago when I received a fund-raising request that referred to those of us with chronic fatigue syndrome as having wasted lives.

I tripped over the word *wasted*. I had not thought of my life as being wasted in a long time—no matter how debilitating the illness might be. As someone who has raised funds in the nonprofit sector, I understand the tendency to choose vivid, dramatic words to increase the impact of my message. It is believed that if your audience doesn't feel the pain and suffering of the population you're raising money for, they're much less likely to give. The unintended result of that kind of marketing is that it perpetuates stereotypes and distortions that may work against your goals in the long run.

I don't know if that author really meant to suggest that he thought my life was wasted. He may have just been going for impact and grabbed a word that seemed to convey the seriousness of the condition to justify his call to action. That author is not the only person who talks about health in such terms. People say, "If we have our health, we have everything." Inherent in that statement is a belief that the reverse is also true: if we don't have our health, we have nothing. I've known many healthy people who were miserable.

Another mailing advertised publications about wealth and health that declared that wealth doesn't do you any good if you don't have health. I can't imagine that anyone really believes that having money is useless if you have an illness. What better time in one's life to have resources to purchase medical care, nutritious food, equipment, and household items that are comforting and supportive?

As I pondered these word choices, I realized how far I had come in my own thinking about the meaning of being healthy. I had moved from feeling useless, thwarted, and better off dead, to a place of appreciation of all I experienced, achieved, and contributed—sometimes in spite of my illness and sometimes because of it. I know how many people love me and would miss me if I were gone. I remember the beautiful places I've been and so many of the fascinating people I have met.

This isn't a Pollyanna attitude or look-for-the-silver-lining speech, trying to make sense and meaning out of pain and suffering. This is an observation of what has actually transpired in my life. It's mechanical. *This happened, and I made that choice. I went in that direction or met so-and-so or developed my understanding of this or that.* I can tangibly see (like George Bailey at the end of the perennially favorite movie, *It's a Wonderful Life*) that my being on the planet has had value. It is not the life I envisioned when I was young—and I have not accomplished the things I used to imagine were essential for earning my way into God's graces—but it is not even close to being a wasted life. Waking up to the truth of my life's meaning and value wasn't easy, but it was simple. It merely took a change in perception.

In our efforts to understand the extent of our power over reality, we learn that the words we use to describe the reality we want to change—or the reality we want to bring into being—carry a huge amount of power. We may choose certain words because they're commonly used or easily understood by others. Sometimes we pick a word to emphasize a point (as with the author of the fund-raising letter). We often use words because we have come to believe they are true; we may have integrated them so tightly into our being that we are unconscious of them. In that regard, the spiritual concept of consciousness has proven useful for me. It's not just about developing more consciousness about what's happening in the present moment. It's also about being aware, observing the things I do and say, and noticing how well they serve or don't serve me. My language needed a lot of work, and it takes continued commitment to replace certain words with others that make life work better for me.

Many people are writing their stories of awakening as a result of life-threatening or chronic illnesses, life-altering injuries, or losing loved ones. The awakening is usually about the realization of how important it is to appreciate and pay attention to what you have in the present moment—to really *be* with what and who you have in your life. People say these illnesses and injuries have been gifts, but sometimes they apologize for suggesting that such painful experiences could be gifts. The idea has become such a cliché that the truth becomes insignificant. Maybe we don't need to say that something is a blessing in disguise because it's not really in disguise if we look at it with wisdom. I came to see my chronic illness as a gift and a blessing, and then it deepened into something more fundamental.

Many years ago, I read a report about a celebrity that has never left me. Someone had asked her if she *had to* perform that night. She said she used to think that way until she began to think about all the people who were also getting dressed and would be leaving their homes and driving to watch her performance. In a flash, she shifted her view. She realized that she would *get to* perform that evening.

That story made me aware that I used the expression *have to* to describe many things in my life. *I have to wash the dishes. I have to go to work. I have to go to the doctor.* It's certainly how I felt about my illness: *I have to live with this.* As it happens, I am going to the dentist today to have an abscessed tooth extracted. I don't *have* to go. No one is standing over me with a whip. I am choosing to go because I prefer not to deal with the consequences of not going. To think that I *have* to go moves me back into child mode. That would mean I am no longer in charge of my life, although I am an adult physically and mentally. As a child, I did things to please others because I had no power. I was dependent upon the goodwill of others because they had all the power.

When I started to understand the power that words held to change my experience with reality, I knew I wanted to shift some of my phrases. By substituting the words *have to* with *get to* or *choose to,* I stay in my own power and authority. I am not whipsawed by events and the opinions of others.

I acknowledge that my life is a gift and a privilege. I *get to* live this life. I have experienced things that no one else has experienced in exactly the same way. I have learned things, gained insights, and explored terrain that I would not have been able to without the chronic illness I used to think of as tragedy. That doesn't make my experience special. It makes it unique—just as every other person's journey is unique. It's not a badge of honor. It's an appreciation, a sense of gratitude that I've been able to explore caverns and caves that without the illness, I wouldn't have even known were there.

Would I prefer to be well and have no pain or fatigue? Of course I would. It's an odd paradox that comes through the lens of having had the experience. With consciousness, these kinds of distinctions become clearer. We can appreciate the beauty of snow and ice and at the same time prefer that the roads weren't too slick to drive on them. Learning the difference between preferring and being invested in something being a certain way helps a great deal with accepting reality. When we expect things to turn out like we want them to, we can spend a lot of time in disappointment and frustration.

I want to appreciate the people and things in my life today because I get to experience and explore them—whether they give me pleasure or pain. If it's here *for now*, there's a reason for it. If it's something I want to try to change, I am free to make plans and take steps. Having the power to deal with any situation starts with recognizing and accepting where things are right now.

We use other powerful words and expressions that not only reflect our beliefs but also shape our beliefs. For example, words such as *everybody, nothing, everything, never,* and *always* and concepts such as *all or nothing* pack a deep wallop on our psyches in both important and mundane matters. The idea that everybody's doing it or everybody's wearing it may help us as teenagers who are trying to find our identities. As adults, we know that it's not true that everybody is doing anything. However, we often measure others and ourselves against this nebulous belief because it's in our unconscious.

In the realm of people with disabilities and health conditions, there are many stereotypes: They're all less able than nondisabled people. Everyone with a psychiatric condition is a mass murderer. All people on disability benefits are milking the system. Those of us with chronic illnesses may be tempted to say, "Nobody understands me," "Nothing ever helps," or "I'll always have to struggle."

On today's local news, a woman with cancer stated, "You can never give up." Not giving up may be what that person's soul is exploring, but sometimes quitting is not only an option—it may be the perfect path for some people. If that's the choice they prefer, they're not failures if they decide to stop treatment and accept whatever course the cancer takes.

It would be really interesting if someone on television said, "I've tried all the treatments that I have the energy, resources, and interest in trying. I am at peace now." Rather than judging our choices because someone declared that the only valid response is to never give up, perhaps we could ask, "What is relevant for my soul's path?" This can move the discussion out of the realm of giving up or not giving up.

Some souls are exploring consciously living effectively with cancer. Other souls are having experiences with faith healing. And some are interested in the experience of going through different kinds of treatments for the sake of the experience itself.

Many people use the phrase that someone *lost her battle* with cancer. That phrase says two things to me: a) life is a war that must be fought rather than an adventure to be experienced, and b) the person who died was a loser. Since we all die, are we all losers?

Another curious thing is when someone says, "These migraine headaches are ruining my life." Really? When I look at that person, I see the rich tapestry of her accomplishments, her interesting and loving personality, and the equally talented and loving family that surrounds her. Another way of looking at it might be to say, "These migraines are a significant factor I must consider as I negotiate my way through the day."

As consciousness on the planet is shifting about who we really are, our language is naturally shifting as well. As more conscious beings, we can proactively choose to stop using words that disempower or move us away from our true essence. We can substitute words that empower us and move us into alignment with our true Selves. Each of us can examine our own language and note the words and phrases that would be useful to let go of.

Instead of saying, "I brought this pain on myself by overdoing it," perhaps we can say, "I'm going to set some priorities for today so I can use my energy wisely." We can notice how we feel when we use certain words or phrases. How do certain words affect us energetically? How do we behave when we use various words? How do words shape what we believe about ourselves? As grown-ups, we get to choose many things, and the words we use are some of the most potentially life-altering things we have control over.

With perspective on my long-standing illness, I can see that everything about it has not been horrible. I'm not miserable every minute. A great deal of it has been annoying and tedious, but my whole life has not been catastrophic. Every part of my body doesn't hurt. On some days, I have more energy than on other days. On some days, I feel reasonably well. On some days, I accomplish everything on my to-do list. On some days, I only accomplish a few things.

Using accurate words enhances my capacity to accept what is real, to let go of what is not real, and to stay in the present. Words carry extraordinary power to liberate us from—or bind us to—limiting beliefs.

CHAPTER 15

Lather, Rinse, Repeat

Software Instructions: Just push the doohickey button and follow the instructions.

Me: Where is the doohickey button?

Software Instructions: [silence]

Me: Maybe I can find the answer in the Help File.

Help File: Just push the doohickey button and follow the instructions.

Me: Maybe I can find the answer online.

Online Chat: The doohickey button is next to the whatzit.

Me: Argh!

A central theme of my journey has been the feeling that I am speaking Klingon when I try to communicate about my chronic illness. In turn, it has felt like others were speaking an unintelligible language when I've searched for help. The experience I relayed above with software happens when there's a disconnect between how techno-nerds think and how techno-impaired people process information. Experts know their information, but they may not necessarily know how to instruct others in that information. They may make assumptions, skip over critical details, or even operate out of a desire not to insult the more advanced user.

As a person with a complicated and unusual set of health issues, I have felt challenged to convey my experiences and needs to others. I've read the volumes of material on theories, treatments, and healing over the years, but I've struggled to understand how to apply much of the medical and technical information and recommendations.

I saw a woman with fibromyalgia on a television talk show recently who wanted to get some help communicating with her husband because he didn't believe she was sick. The husband thought that she was just making up her symptoms to get out of doing the things she didn't want to do. I was mesmerized to see another person with invisible chronic illness reporting that she was not taken seriously by a key person in her life.

I especially felt a kinship with her when she indicated that she knew what kind of person she *could* be if she didn't have the condition. She hadn't yet been able to declare what was real in that moment and say, "Today my limitations are ABC; my abilities are XYZ." This seems to be a place that many of us with invisible chronic illnesses start. Since it's invisible, it also seems intangible. We may keep thinking about the person we used to be or imagine how we would be if we didn't have pain and fatigue. Our explanations are muddled. It takes time and practice to figure out the language to describe our situations and needs to people who have never experienced what we're experiencing.

As someone who has been able to keep working in spite of how sick I often am, I used to struggle with a feeling of unfairness in the work environment. Coworkers who experience similar symptoms when they come down with an illness will take time off. If I took every day off that I felt that level of illness, I would probably lose my job. I continue to move forward because I love my work. I've figured out how to build rest periods into my days. It's amazing what one can accomplish from a horizontal position in this age of electronics.

I also used to want sympathy, but then I realized it was asking a great deal of others to provide that for me. It's not anyone else's job to provide me with sympathy. It's also asking a great deal of someone to sustain a degree of sympathy for something that is continuous and not easily understood, particularly if I keep trying to be cheerful and say I'm fine when someone asks. And if I'm operating from the principle that I should accomplish all the things on my list that day, rather than doing what I can, I confuse other people and myself.

Because having sympathy and understanding mattered to me at one time, my relationships and friendships often felt off-kilter. No one seemed to be able to live up to my nebulous expectations. The solution was to have acceptance of myself, which led to the more neutral place of asking for accommodations and clear communication. Then it became irrelevant whether anyone was sympathetic because the point was to have a life that worked for me—not to fill an emotional void. One of the results of that shift is that I now feel supported in my work, although there is rarely any discussion about my health or limitations. Having an understanding about my boundaries and what works for me make such discussion rarely necessary.

Many of us with chronic illness entrap ourselves by worrying about making other people feel guilty. They often don't know much about our health because we withhold information. It's tiresome to keep saying, "I feel terrible today!" or "I've got such and such going on today." Some of us would much rather just say, "I'm fine," and move on instead of having to use the energy to explain.

The husband of the person with fibromyalgia mentioned above made the point that his wife would sometimes rush around doing things and other times would claim she was not able to do anything. He was not able to make sense out of that because if she were really sick, how could she accomplish so much at certain times? This is a common challenge for people who experience fluctuating energy, pain, or mental clarity.

Amina Donna Kruck is a colleague at Arizona Bridge to Independent Living in Phoenix. She is vice president of advocacy and experiences chronic illness. She said, "Having a chronic illness makes you an opportunist. You wait for a door to open and then you run like hell."[22] I understood perfectly when she said it, but I wondered how many people in the room could relate to what she was saying. Like the husband of the woman with fibromyalgia, even when you live with someone who's behaving that way, you may be bewildered by it.

Sometimes it seems to be a surprise to people I've known for a long time when I say I don't feel well enough to do something. They act as if they had never heard before that I have a chronic illness. There have been some people who were genuinely shocked by the news—even though I had mentioned it several times. Sometimes I think the information doesn't sink in because I keep participating as fully as I can, as often as I can. Some people forget about the illness or believe I must have gotten well.

These breakdowns in understanding with friends, family members, and coworkers can trigger emotional hurt and resentment. They are opportunities (there's that word again) to get clear about our own needs and to share the essentials with key people—when it's relevant—to take care of ourselves. There is no other person who can ever fully understand our personal experiences with chronic illness—even if they've been through a chronic illness themselves. They may have a greater understanding, but they can never know precisely what our experiences have been.

One of the fundamental characteristics of an empowered person is being able to speak your own truth. There is no doctor, close friend, or expert author who can ever know how much effort it takes us to do something or what it costs us to do it. And more importantly, they cannot know what we should or shouldn't do. There is no one else on the planet with our precise set of circumstances, temperament, genetics, and experiences. And no one else has the authority to determine our personal path (unless we've had our legal rights removed by a court or are in a coma—and even some of the guardianship rulings are not necessary when individual skills are evaluated from a human rights perspective).

The really exciting news is that we don't have to be understood by *everyone*. First of all, we don't have enough energy and time to make ourselves understood by everyone. Second, it doesn't matter if the vast majority of people get what we're dealing with. And third, it would be tiresome to most other people to hear us repeating the litany of our symptoms.

Even people in our inner circles who are vital to our well-being don't have to understand all the details of how our bodies and minds work and how every moment of our time is affected.

How could someone who's never experienced FM, CFS, or MCS fully understand the complex web of interconnected things we experience? How could they precisely know the implications of the cascade of symptoms where one thing after another malfunctions?

FM, CFS, and MCS are rather strange conditions. It may be difficult to comprehend what it's like to have muscles and joints that hurt all the time. Mental confusion and attention deficit issues are trickier still to convey. Severe, constant fatigue might not make sense to those who find a night's sleep refreshing, and the business about having energy right now and very little ten minutes later is bewildering to anyone who has never experienced it.

Finding examples of things that are within the realm of someone's experience can be helpful. Many people can relate to what the flu and muscle strain feel like, so we might be able to use those things for comparison. If you do not have FM, CFS, or MCS, but you love someone who does and want to understand better what they're going through, wait until the next time you have the flu, are hungover from drinking too much, take a sleep aid and awaken groggy, or overextend with exercise and hurt all over. Imagine what your life would be like if you felt like that all the time. It's not a precise match for what your loved one is experiencing, but it may give you additional insight into what it may be like to be sick every day.

For those of us with chronic illness, we might consider making a list of the significant people who could make our lives easier if they understood *enough* about what we're experiencing and how we want to convey that information; and then take steps to communicate it to them. Since I do much better with the written word than with spoken explanations, I often use e-mail or letters when I want to describe things I get emotionally charged about. I can be more deliberate (and sensible) about the words I choose. That's not always possible, but when verbal discussion is required, I remember that I can go back later and share a clarification if I feel I didn't explain something as I would have liked or if the other person doesn't seem to get it. Having the option of a do-over is a great gift of the universe.

Many of the communication issues I experienced with people who are most important to me cleared up dramatically when I learned to say, "I can do this, but I can't do that," or "Which of the things that you're asking of me really matter to you so I can set some priorities for my energy and abilities?" It is often a matter of simply being proactive.

When I stopped blaming people for not understanding, it was such a relief. I stopped stewing in that kind of victimhood. I realized that I was doing people a favor by giving them accurate information about what was reasonable to expect from me. Figuring out what worked let me be clear in my communications. I decided to start giving people the benefit of the doubt. I started believing that, on some level, people did not want me to be in pain. More specifically, they wanted to believe that I was not in pain when they were trying to get me to do something. When I know something is likely to be problematic for me, I try to remember to give the other person the responsibility of knowing that what they're asking of me will cause me problems—and could be problematic for them.

I would like others to understand three things: 1) I don't feel good most of the time, but I don't have the energy to keep saying it over and over so others will remember; 2) I want certain accommodations and adaptations to make my life work more smoothly and easily; and 3) my life is not diminished by the illness—it's diminished by not having necessary accommodations.

When someone suggests my symptoms aren't real, it is an opportunity to check in with my own truth. From a soul perspective, how other people perceive my illness may act as a laboratory for exploring my feelings and the psychological aspect of illness. It also provides fodder for logistical creativity, as I recognize the choices I now have because I've learned from others' reactions.

Having a health condition has taught me to trust myself, and it has taught me that I play a critical part in other people's understanding. I have to give them accurate information. It is my responsibility to know the information so I can relay it. I also have the responsibility to not be invested in the outcome of the communication. I am not responsible for how someone else feels or reacts. I cannot be free if I go up and down like a yo-yo, depending upon whether things are going a certain way in a given moment.

I can't focus on the way the other person is responding. I have to focus on being clear and fair and saying what I really mean. That way, my confusion and fear will diminish.

Shifting my focus helps me own reality as it is right now and not apologize for things I have no control over. If I do these things, it increases the chances that we all can win.

My cognitive challenges have been the most difficult to communicate and have caused the most emotional pain when another person jumps to inaccurate conclusions. Sometimes my attention difficulties are interpreted as not being interested in the other person. Some people are frustrated when I'm not processing what they're saying or if I don't remember things. When I was buying an expensive product a few years ago, one of the sales reps launched into a rapid-fire speech about an extended warranty. He talked so fast that I didn't grasp anything he said. I asked him to start over, slow down, and repeat what he had said while I took notes. He seemed impatient at my request, but I felt a sense of accomplishment that I had learned how to take care of myself in that way. Having the information I needed to make an important and expensive decision was more important to me than the opinion of a stranger.

These are the kind of behaviors that began to shift for me as I gained a sense of empowerment. There was a time when I believed that taking care of me in such ways was a selfish act— that my purpose on Earth was to take care of other people's feelings and needs regardless of how they affected me. Like many others, I concluded that it was expected and appropriate to pass out rather than put on my oxygen mask first because the other person's life was more important than my own. Learning that taking care of myself is not selfishness was hard for me.

Empowerment does not mean that we treat other people disrespectfully. It means that we treat ourselves respectfully, and in doing so, we establish clear boundaries for what works for us—and what doesn't.

It has been challenging to communicate my needs to people who matter to me emotionally. It took longer to find the courage and the words to be clear and constructive. I know it can be frustrating for the other person to give information to someone who doesn't process incoming information in the same way that they do. I can let them know there are two things that are helpful to me: patience and repetition. It's not their job to guess whether I'm having an off day with my cognitive abilities. I can choose to tell them or not tell them, but I am no longer insulted when they repeat things or talk more slowly. I may stop participating in the conversation if the other person implies that I'm being stupid. When I feel wounded, my ability to communicate effectively diminishes.

Taking the time to process what happened and writing to people rather than calling them works better for me. If a person matters enough to me, I will work through it. If he or she doesn't matter in that way, I don't use up my limited energy trying to fix things. When I say that someone doesn't matter, I don't mean that I don't care about him or her as a human being. I mean that the person's opinion of me is irrelevant to making my life work. Having a personal commitment to communicate my needs up front and work through communication breakdowns with people who matter has resulted in way fewer hurt feelings and resentments.

One of the other slippery slopes for those of us with invisible chronic illness is feeling guilty and apologizing for things we have no control over. It's like saying, "I'm sorry I couldn't make the sun shine today." I used to apologize for everything, especially for not feeling well enough to participate in activities. Apologizing inappropriately made me feel disempowered and small, and I didn't notice whether my apologies were relevant to the other people. Then I learned there was a difference between saying, "I'm sorry that I disappointed you today," and "I'm sorry that you were disappointed."

The first apology assumes the illness is my fault. The second apology is still an authentic apology—but not for my limitations. I do care that the other person is disappointed, but I'm not responsible for the disappointment. If the other person says, "But we were so counting on you," I remember that kind of response is more about the other person than about me. Someone else might say, "We missed you, but we're really glad you took care of yourself." That's more comforting to hear, but neither of those responses has anything to do with whether I will choose to participate or not participate. Taking care of me is my priority and my responsibility.

Sometimes we define friendship as doing things for the other person. In the absence of things being done, one might conclude there's no genuine friendship. Friends who can't accept that I won't always answer the phone just because it's them calling (who would have ever thought that caller ID could be a disability accommodation?), send a birthday card every year without fail, or engage in lengthy phone calls have moved out of my circle. If we define friendship as holding someone in a loving space in our hearts and minds rather than being available at the person's every beck and call, we will have a different quality of friendships. We will also have a different quality of life for ourselves.

Several of my closest friends understand how tiring phone calls are for me, and they know I will call them back when I have the energy. Some of my friends are energized by talking, so it's a true act of friendship for them to accept this kind of boundary as part of how we interact.

Relationships depend a great deal on the quality of communication. By coming into full relationship with ourselves, we can offer honest and useful communication with others. For anyone who is wondering whether you can keep a marriage or relationship together while managing a chronic illness, especially if you feel judged and dismissed by the other person, asking a different question might be more useful. Ask how you can strengthen the relationship with yourself so that you are acting from a place of personal power and congruence. This may help answer the other question.

CHAPTER 16

Writing Different Stories

I n the *Star Trek: The Next Generation* episode "The Masterpiece Society," a community of humans who were genetically engineered to be perfect live in an artificial environment on the planet Moab IV. Each person in the society has been selectively bred to play a specific part—leader, scientist, musician, teacher, male, female, or whatever the society needs them to be—to keep the society working in perfect precision. Genetic defects, disabilities, and other so-called imperfections are not allowed as part of the society. After eight generations of unspoiled equilibrium, the society becomes confronted with imminent annihilation by an approaching stellar core fragment.

The Federation starship *Enterprise*, commanded by Captain Jean-Luc Picard, passes by, detects the danger to the planet, and opens communication with the society. This sets in motion another kind of potential destruction, unforeseen and morally questionable—or so it seems. *Enterprise* personnel beam down to the society to assist the citizens in shoring up their defenses against the fragment. The society is shaken to its foundation by the introduction of a new consciousness about different ways of living and being.

Enterprise Chief Engineer Geordi LaForge has been blind since birth. He was assigned to work with the colony's leading scientist to adjust the path of the core fragment. After several unsuccessful attempts, Geordi realizes that the only technology that will save the colony is the same type of technology that makes his visor work. The visor is an adaptive device that he wears over his eyes to see. The irony is that the solution to saving this society of perfect people lies in technology that was created for someone who would have never existed if he had been conceived on that world. The citizens of the colony had grown up with the story that their definition of perfection and purpose was the only acceptable one.

There is an interesting contradiction that often happens in the human experience: we deny things that are true and make up stories about other things and believe that they're true. It's not because there's something wrong with us that we do this. It's the way our brains are wired until we figure out that we have the option and the capacity to rewire them. We don't know that we're making up stories and believing they're true until we stop and notice what we're doing—like the day I was searching the Internet for ways to kill myself.

After years of counseling, personal coaching, reading hundreds of books, attending myriad workshops, and suffering with emotional and physical pain, why was that moment different? I can't know for sure. It's not the sort of thing that's easily measured. I just know that by that point in my process, I had come to understand that I was much larger than my illness, my history, and my stories. Without any analysis, I looked at my thoughts another way and knew that thoughts of killing myself were just another story. I knew that I had options for dealing with the challenges of my life, but I didn't know any of it—until I knew it.

One of the places I used to make up self-limiting stories was around the authority and power that I believed doctors had over me. Even after I became an adult, I continued to feel like a dependent child in the presence of doctors. I had a breakthrough one day when a doctor was chastising me for a decision I had made. I was able to push back—with the voice of an adult and without anger—by explaining why I had made the choice and telling him that I stood by the decision. I was beginning to let go of the story that he was more powerful than I was. I left the appointment soaring because my newfound voice had come to me by making up a different story. It changed my definition of the power of an authority figure. It was not a dismissal of medical expertise; it was a starting place for me to claim the authority and power that were already mine.

I had been wandering in circles and believing that I was supposed to behave differently. I thought I had to please other people for my soul's salvation. I had focused on being adequate so I could have their approval. I thought I had been focusing on being well. I couldn't see the distinction between those two things until I saw it. I could only allow it to percolate within me until it was ready to emerge as a tangible shift.

We make up stories for all sorts of reasons. It's part of the human game. Fear may be one of the most powerful generators of stories. In the realm of fear, people with traditional disabilities are often afraid of stigma. Because others recognize that the person with a disability is different, and assumptions are made about capabilities and potential behaviors, the person with the disability may easily become afraid that everyone is going to label and stigmatize him or her. Expectations for failure set up by parents, teachers, medical practitioners, and service providers are much more common for people with disabilities than those who are nondisabled. Many people with significant disabilities have been placed in institutions because their families or doctors believed they were a burden or menace and could not contribute to society. In recent years, many of those individuals have been given opportunities to live in the community, hold jobs, and demonstrate the capacity to be full citizens. Society has been writing different stories.

Some people with disabilities carry fear about retaliation because of what they've experienced when they've reported mistreatment or abuse by caregivers. They may have lost their care altogether and been left in life-threatening situations. I've known several individuals who have experienced such things. Because of what happened in the past, some individuals live with the belief that the world is an unsafe place and fear that they will be abused again.

People with certain invisible chronic illnesses are often fearful of not being heard and not being believed. A natural consequence of not being believed is not getting the medical care or emotional support you want and need. For many years, I was afraid I was going to die—either by my own hand because of despair or by what I considered the failure of the medical system. When I started unraveling my fear, I found layers of things that I was afraid would happen. I was amazed when I finally grasped how deeply fear was embedded in my DNA.

What does the absence of fear look like? How can you not be afraid when you know that what actually happened is real and could easily happen again—when you see people with disabilities who have been shunned, locked up in institutions, abused, made to leave restaurants because their presence offended other patrons, involuntarily sterilized, forced to undergo treatments they don't want, or killed in the name of ethnic cleansing? How do you find trust when you hear stories about people with extreme chemical sensitivities who are living in tents, cars, and cages in the woods? What about the stories of marriages or relationships breaking up because one of the partners doesn't want to deal with the challenges of a sick spouse? What about when people comment about how dreadful or fruitless your life must be because you have a disability or illness? How do you not move into a grasping mode, reaching for every shred of power you can find to have some control over your destiny?

Running from fear may not be a game we can win. It's a natural part of the human experience. It's not a war between our finite selves and our souls. When we realize that what we're experiencing isn't a punishment, a sign of a defect, or a reflection of our goodness or badness, trusting the moment starts to make a lot of sense. By trusting that our souls played a role in choosing the characteristics and circumstances of our lives, we are able to remember that we have more creative possibilities than we thought. By trusting our souls on a moment-by-moment basis to support us in making life choices, we can manage our illnesses more easily. When we're differently abled, we have opportunities to access our creativity, intellect, and souls in a way we might not have otherwise. It's an interesting and stimulating opportunity—not a tragedy.

We've done a lot of thinking and talking about fear. Judging ourselves for being afraid can be a bigger problem than the fear itself. We can use tools, such as meridian tapping, that are available for dealing with fear, trauma, and knee-jerk reactions. They can be powerfully effective in reducing anxiety and worry.

Tools are only one part of the equation for me. By changing my beliefs about disability and chronic illness—from a defect, failing, or abnormality to an aspect of diversity—I was able to create new stories. We will always have our stories—no matter how we change them—but it's useful to remember that new ways of thinking about disabilities and chronic illnesses are still just stories. There's nothing wrong with having our beliefs and attitudes, but as we become more conscious of what's real and what's true, we begin to notice our stories and where we can change our minds and take new directions that help us get to where we really want to go. A large part of my journey has been about sifting and sorting the truth, and my journey continues because I relish having more joy in my life.

The journey with fear has been one of the greatest teachers of my life. I don't begrudge the experience. It prepared me for a delicious experience with trust when I finally realized that I could have it. I trust my soul, others, the universe, and life. I can keep making up stories about how awful my life is if I really want to. I'm skillful at storytelling. I've had a lot of practice, but I don't enjoy being terrified anymore. I get much more enjoyment out of seeing reality as it is for now—and believing that all is well.

CHAPTER 17

Trusting Self

The disability rights and independent living movements are on to something dynamic. Each soul is precious and of the same worth as every other soul—regardless of how different the vessels that carry the souls look or act. No matter how disfigured they are. No matter how many body parts are missing—or how much they drool, slur their words, stagger as they walk, talk to entities others cannot see, or depend upon medical equipment—each soul has its own game plan.

You're not a fool, you're not stupid, and you're not a reject because your body gives out or your brain takes a vacation at seemingly inopportune moments. So what if others don't know it or acknowledge it? Your soul cannot be denied what it came to Earth to do. That point of view has taught me a great deal about self-trust.

Having worked in the disability field as long as I have, I know about a variety of medical conditions and disabilities. If I were to continue to search for a more definitive diagnosis, I could imagine several conditions being plausible for myself. I could keep spending money, energy, and time. I've become an expert at that.

I can see that my addiction to the search for answers was an aspect of the journey that led me to understand what and who I can trust. Learning to trust myself has taught me that I will know what I need to know, in each moment, to make the best decisions about treatments and protocols. That's not a declaration that I never intend to consult with health care professionals again. The way I frame life in partnership with soul has nothing to do with what health care professionals can or cannot do.

By working in partnership with my soul, I trust that I will know when a consultation with a health practitioner is warranted. This isn't playing Russian roulette with my health or being whimsical. There is no one more committed to my health than I am, and I intend to stay as healthy as I can. I consider the treatments and protocols I've read about or talked to practitioners about, and then I pay attention to what's in front of me. I listen to my inner guidance about what's real and relevant. It's simple. It's mechanical. I recently went through some major medical procedures that I will be paying off for some time. The decision to go through them came after a year of considering the value and potential side effects. There are no guarantees that I would have improved health after going through them, and the financial impact was heavy, so I did not take it lightly. But I reached a point of feeling resolved and satisfied with my decision.

I've also realized how capable I am of making more routine choices on a day-to-day basis about what I eat, what environments I go into, what supplements I take, how much rest I need, and how I deal with my emotions. It no longer matters to me in the larger sense what the scientific data suggests.

After I've read the research and considered its relevance for me, I base decisions about my body, health, and lifestyle on what I believe is true for me—and what will help make my life work. If something about an option seems off, I listen to that intuition. I don't need to have scientific proof that low-level exposures to chemicals are harmful to me. I am not a "nutcase" if I choose not to breathe or eat formaldehyde, phenol, petrochemicals, PCBs, and organophosphates—regardless of how low the levels are. I am comfortable saying to the so-called experts who proclaim that I have imagined my body's reactions to chemicals, "I am as bewildered by your willingness to breathe, drink, and eat toxic substances as you are by my unwillingness to do so." I have the authority to choose what I think is in my best interest. Others can label me in any way they want, but I no longer accept their pronouncements of what I *should* prefer for myself. It may be a strategic ploy or a great marketing tool to label me a weirdo because I want clean air, water, and food, but it's no longer working. This is a philosophy that was beyond my reach during the years I believed that all the answers to life and the universe could be found with other people.

How does one transition from believing that your life is a waste to trusting it to unfold perfectly? It can't simply be a matter of changing your belief about that, can it? I no longer think that it's about working harder, better, smarter, or longer. I believe it's about recognizing who we are and accepting that we are already all we were meant to be. I know that seems contradictory.

If our true essence is Spirit, which we think of as perfection, how can all these imperfections we see be all that we were meant to be? Shouldn't we keep striving for health, wholeness, correcting our flaws, and plugging the holes of deficiency? There's a vast difference between pursuing these things because we believe there's something wrong with us and allowing ourselves to awaken to greater consciousness as a natural unfolding process. We become more awake, more centered, and happier as we trust our Selves, but the absence of consciousness previously doesn't mean we were defective. We came here to experience the human game, and every characteristic and circumstance is part of a particular path.

After decades of enjoying *The Wizard of Oz* over and over again, it dawned on me that Dorothy could go home again because she never actually left. She didn't blow it because she thought she left Kansas. It was only because she thought she left Kansas that she got scared. She could never leave her soul, and her soul wouldn't leave her. She could, however, shift her perspective and realize she was always home, even when she was exploring. Home is wherever the soul is.

The changes in my life have not been the result of hocus-pocus or woo-woo activity. Most of the time, they were the result of taking one step at a time toward what I wanted to bring into being. When I wanted to get out of debt, saying affirmations may have opened up my energy field for accepting abundance, dispelling blocks placed by my distorted sense of what I deserve, but on a practical level, spending less and saving more got me out of debt. It was mechanical. Sometimes things come into our lives that we don't consciously envision and work toward because unseen forces are working behind the scenes. It's still mechanical. It's just not readily apparent.

We can trust that things are unfolding as they should, that if we ask for guidance it will be given, and that whatever seems negative are merely steps toward getting what we want. They are opportunity portals. We can trust that the universe is supporting us 100 percent of the time and trust that our own souls are taking care of us.

There is an image about trust from a movie I especially love. It became timeless for me because it was so powerful. In the third Indiana Jones movie, *The Last Crusade*, Indiana is in search of the Holy Grail. To get to the temple carved out of rock—where an ancient knight protects the Holy Grail— Indiana must cross over a chasm that appears to have no way across. Indiana falters until he recalls the instruction that he must have faith to be successful in claiming the Holy Grail. I think of the spiritual lesson in terms of trust rather than faith because even though the dictionary definitions of faith and trust are similar, *faith* has become charged with doctrinal meaning for many of us.

The definition of trust that I like to work with and that I have chosen to apply in the Indiana Jones scenario is belief that someone or something is reliable.[23] Indiana is visibly afraid of falling. He remembers the instruction written in his father's archeology notebook about having faith. He picks up a handful of dirt and throws it out over the chasm, and it sticks to an unseen footbridge that is right in front of his feet. The bridge that was there all along becomes visible. When Indiana believes he will be supported, he sees the evidence that he already is.

Striving to stop negative emotions and achieve perfect health to prove my worth is a bottomless pit because I can never be good enough from that perspective. I was so relieved when I realized the value of spiritual practice is not trying to win the approval of God. When I start to get fearful, I gently shift my focus and see that the bridge is always there.

CHAPTER 18

*Unwrapping
the Gift*

My four decades in the world of disability have allowed me to meet thousands of people with disabilities and chronic illnesses. Some of the conditions many of the people live with are so significant and profound that their limitations may make other people wonder how the individuals could continue living—much less working and participating in community life.

Everyone I've met who stays open to possibilities has figured out a way to make their lives work: creatively dealing with extreme speech impairments, being almost totally paralyzed, having severe fatigue that requires continual bed rest, or managing the voices in their heads. One does not have to physically speak, walk, see, hear, or share the same reality as others to have meaningful relationships and life pursuits. What more brilliant way for Spirit to explore time and space, limits and boundaries than through physical and mental variations?

I see opportunities in my fatigue every day. It allows me to pace myself and let go of the myriad things I don't have the energy to deal with (and that don't really matter anyway). The pain sharpens my focus because it reminds me to breathe deeply and move my body in a certain way to lessen the impact of the pain. It highlights the pleasure of a long, hot soaking bath, the sun's warm rays, or a massage. The gifts never seem to end.

There is a Japanese concept that I ran across recently called *wabi-sabi*. I had never heard of it before, but I found it delightfully relevant for what I wanted to convey about the perfection in disability and chronic illness. Wabi-sabi is about finding beauty in so-called imperfection; in fact, the imperfection is seen to add value to the thing that has the imperfection. A tree damaged by lightning, for example, becomes a new work of art with its limbs broken in a particular way. With this definition, the person with a disability or chronic illness has value added *because* of the condition.

In the disability rights and independent living movements, we've repeatedly witnessed transformation in individuals who realize that their disabilities are tickets into a society that prizes the differences. Thousands of individuals are embraced as one of us in a way that many people with disabilities have never experienced before. These experiences can bring the same kind of healing energy that "black is beautiful" did for the civil rights movement.

Many believe that there is purpose in life, and some even say there is a reason for everything that happens—even things labeled *tragic* or *catastrophic*—but at the same time, many people continue to consider illness and disability as indicators that we are not yet spiritually evolved. Illness and disability somehow got stored in a different cubbyhole for many—even those of us who saw purpose in life. The belief runs deep that we have failed in some way if we have such conditions, that we are suffering victims, and that our lives are diminished.

We created a rather complicated explanation for acute illness, chronic illness, and disability in our process of creating reality. From sin and God's wrath to karma, from negative thinking to psychological problems, from the toxic environment to genetics, from poor lifestyle and eating habits to bad parenting, and from poverty to the lack of health care workers in certain geographic areas, we have woven a web of reasons, definitions, and cures to satisfy our longing for answers. The new age movement has added chakras being out of balance and leaking power, past lives, and other people's psychic energy draining us.

Many of us with chronic illnesses tell ourselves we're not trying hard enough, we're not worthy of being well, the universe is out to get us, corporate greed is harming us, and life's a bitch and then we die. Others may tell us we enjoy being sick, we're full of repressed feelings, we're trying to get out of sex, we're getting back at our parents, we want to get out of work, and we don't believe enough that we will be healed. The internal and external chatter can be exhausting around chronic illness, and that chatter becomes the problem rather than the illness.

I believe the reason for chronic illness is much simpler. To me, illnesses, disabilities, and diseases are simply mechanisms for a soul's journey in the physical realm—some of the tangible vehicles that allow the energetic, spiritual, physical, and mental aspects of our being to interface and permit the journey to take place. They give us tools to recognize and then manage our spiritual power. They are not bad or good, right or wrong. They happen *to* us to have an opportunity *for* us to explore and acquire the results our souls want. They do not make us deficient. They provide Spirit with an avenue to explore dimensions that could not be explored in exactly the same way through other avenues. Any other explanation for illness, disease, and disability tells us somebody did something wrong or we are defective.

That is not to say that because there is purpose in illness and disability, we shouldn't seek medical assistance or search for remedies to help us relieve pain and live healthier and happier lives—or help each other. There is a rapidly expanding array of options for us these days to support our wellbeing. We live in a wondrous time of possibilities. The choices we make become part of the journey, and the experimentation and exploration may be exactly what our souls came here to do. Chronic illness has certainly been a central feature of my education in where and how I can find the nurturing care I resented losing out on as a child. Recognizing that I am my own mother and father—and I am responsible for treating myself lovingly and protectively—gave me the parenting I longed for. The illness led me to that understanding. If you don't have someone in your life who loves you in the way you would like to be cherished, what better circumstance is there to learn to cherish yourself?

Many of us in the physical realm are having so much fun playing with limits and boundaries and time and space that we don't want to be bothered with taking care of ourselves. Self-care can seem rather boring to some who just want to play. One of the outcomes that may result through illness, though, is that we come squarely up against the limits of our bodies. We decide to choose ways of eating, thinking, relating, and living that allow us to have more enjoyment with our emotional, mental, and physical experiences. However, feeling well doesn't necessarily mean that we have discovered the secret to salvation. If I wake up tomorrow and discover that I am cured, I don't believe that means there was something wrong with me all along. The miraculous healing doesn't prove that I have now been *fixed*.

There was a time I would have rejected the spiritual teachings of notable teachers such as Ram Dass because he experienced a stroke and subsequent paralysis. And there have been a number of other spiritual leaders who have died of cancer, heart disease, and other conditions. I couldn't fathom how it was possible for someone to be truly spiritual and have any illness. In a transitional way of thinking, that concept is apparently one that my soul chose to explore for this lifetime because that is the path I have traveled. The experience of illness and disability—regardless of how much faith people have or how conscious they are—makes perfect sense to me now as an ordinary path for any soul to choose for exploration.

If all is Spirit, as we have been exploring in the transitional way of thinking, we are already perfect, but it doesn't automatically enable us to walk on water or cure all sickness. Knowing that some part of us *can* do those things confused me. I assumed that we *should* do those things to prove we know who we really are. Part of my belief about mystical transformation was that we would no longer have any blemishes or physical, mental, or emotional issues.

The point I had missed—because it was part of the hide-and-seek nature of the human game—was that Spirit deliberately set up time and space and limits and boundaries as a laboratory for exploration and creativity. It is not a testing ground to punish or manipulate us. The limitations inherent to the physical experience are treasure boxes to be opened, and their contents used for play.

CHAPTER 19

You Can Relax Now

When you stop worrying about tomorrow and fretting
about yesterday, and you start to understand you're
really safe, you realize there's nothing going wrong here.
All of this is a process. It's a very deliberate and very
specific process. You're not being punished. You're not
being rewarded. You're just being supported through
it. And when that starts to make sense to you, you can
just kind of relax and pay attention and look around.
—Ava Brenner and The Guys[24]

Thinking about my personal journey with illness in a context of a growing planetary consciousness is another way that has helped me to accept and *be* with my condition. Illnesses like FM, CFS, and MCS have had universal impact, not just personal implications for those of us who live with them. These and other so-called 20th century illnesses have by and large not been greatly helped by traditional medical practices. They have contributed significantly to spawning a new breed of health practitioners who practice integrative, complementary, or holistic medicine. Many of these approaches look at an individual as a whole being rather than a symptom or a body part. In essence, they define us not just as living humans, but living souls. They consider a broad range of supports and life changes instead of just pills or surgical procedures. Such approaches may or may not improve our health situations, but they can spur us to find deeper meaning in our lives.

They can also help us recognize our responsibility for our bodies and minds—a significantly empowering process. The days of doctors as all-knowing, all-powerful gods seem to be on the way out. I think the health care crisis in this country reflects the kind of chaos that often happens when old structures are breaking down and new ones are emerging. What seems like a political battle about health insurance might really be a spiritual endeavor that a large percentage of our populace is now ready to embrace. It seems to be providing an incentive for us to find more nurturing models of medical care and new levels of personal commitment for taking care of ourselves.

On an even larger scale, having physical reactions to chemicals and dealing with the effects of toxicity may enable us to think differently about the environment. We can recognize that Earth is a living biological organism that benefits from respect and care just as our bodies do. We experimented with pesticides, herbicides, and toxins in our food, air, and water to see how far we could go with them. Some have believed that food cannot be grown or raised commercially without the addition of such substances and off we went in political battles around that. Some people insisted that chickens must be housed in cramped cages and routinely be given antibiotics; otherwise, it's not possible to make a profit. Others demonstrate that profitability is possible with natural, organic, and nontoxic approaches.

We frame such arguments in political, social, and economic terms, but managing our natural resources with respect is really just an extension of how we value ourselves. When we recognize we are all soul mates because we come from the same Source, we naturally make choices that are healthier and more supportive of ourselves, each other, and our Earth Mother.

To me though, the exploration with chemicals, electromagnetic radiation, mass-production, industrial emissions, food additives, and super-sized meals is part of the same trip to Oz that exploration with illness and disability is part of. We'd might rather say that these things are the result of evil, chaos, punishment, and arbitrary forces; but I am suggesting we look at them again, taking note of the opportunities in them for learning and expanding our consciousness.

If you are the kind of seeker of truth that I have been, you may have explored the concepts that are presented here. By the time I reached my own turning point, I had read hundreds of books, participated in numerous workshops, and tried on different philosophies about the meaning and purpose of creation. I didn't think there was much left that I could learn, but I was still intent on killing myself because I hated my life—right before I had my aha experience. I wasn't stupid, defective, or unspiritual for not previously connecting the dots. I was simply emerging from the fog of ingrained beliefs and attitudes that are, by definition, a part of the human experience. In the realm of disability and chronic illness, when we believe that our conditions are bad or wrong or shouldn't be happening to us, we invest all our energy into trying to make ourselves right.

Within the new view of illness is the recognition that we still may wake up tomorrow and be cured because it's within the realm of possibility. I heard a news report about the success that medical science is having with diminishing allergic reactions to peanuts in children. By the time I finish this manuscript, many things in the world will be different. A key for me was ceasing to expect that things would be as I preferred and accepting them as they are, so that I can explore them—until they are no longer the way they are.

The core of my story has been about figuring out how to accept myself after a troubled childhood wherein I concluded that I was unloved and unlovable. A serious, prolonged illness led me to believe that I was defective, was being punished by

God, and was the victim of a polluted and dangerous planet. My deepest beliefs and understandings have been turned upside down. The journey hasn't been about learning to love myself; it was learning to know who I am. In coming to know who I am, loving myself emerged naturally. In choosing the belief that I am Spirit immersed in a human experience while embracing the concept of accepting all that is, my life began to work in ways I never imagined possible—even when I was avidly pursuing creating another reality.

I'm neurotic sometimes. So what? How clever of me to be strong enough to endure. Bravo! I'm inconsistent, and change my mind sometimes. So what? My body and mind work differently from other bodies and minds on the planet. How interesting. I get angry, sad, frustrated, and discouraged sometimes. Those states are my teachers. Everybody doesn't love me. Why would I want them to? If four hundred other people reject me, yet I accept myself, I have all that I need. Even though I have moments of being neurotic, I deeply and completely accept myself. Even though I still carry traces of shame, I deeply and completely accept myself. Even though multiple body parts are hurting right now, I deeply and completely accept myself.

What might the world look like if we decided to lay down the heavy burden of shoulds that we carry? Borrowing a page from the disability rights movement's playbook, I am not broken because I have chronic health issues or emotional states. I do not need to be fixed. This way of thinking has been a centering point for my own life, helping me to understand that invisible chronic illness is an opportunity to explore, observe, experience, learn, and grow in ways I never could have without the experience.

I have created a new reality, but it's not superior to previous realities. It's not the place of bliss that I used to think was the outcome of consciousness. It's just easier and lighter. I am less distracted by my physical circumstances. I have more of what I believe I want out of life. I have more sense of my inner power and less fear and anxiety. I am less frantic to solve so-called problems—partly because few things are really problems and partly because most things have a way of resolving themselves. If I'm present and take my time to relax and pay attention, I can do everything (or oversee those things I can't do) that really needs to get done.

We may be evolving toward another way of being that will someday allow us to be lighter beings on the physical plane— with less density and more access to our energetic selves. We seem to increasingly recognize our oneness with all things and our equal access to soul power. We may be able to cure all sickness and disability, move matter with our minds, and manifest all sorts of things that we want. There are already people on the planet who seem to have such skills. It's certainly a fun thing to think about and play with. But as we evolve, I don't believe we are becoming more holy or more spiritual. That's part of the hierarchical view of the universe that tells us that whatever we are in this moment is deficient and someday we will be acceptable. Instead, we are merely transitioning to something else.

We have always had direct connection to our souls, but some of us haven't trusted it. Finding the deeper connection with our greater selves is a process for most people, regardless of religious beliefs or conditioning. It isn't a mental process; it is a spiritual one. For many of us, it may need to start on the mental level since we tend to think that all of our knowing is in our minds. Learning to trust that the universe is there for us—and that we're not being punished by the challenges in our lives—may allow us to stop struggling. As we discover how to partner with our souls, we still have the present moment and the existing realities before us. If we take the time and give the attention to explore them, knowing that we are safe, one of the things we can find is freedom from our outmoded beliefs, fears, and discontent about the way things are. All the realities we experience are gifts and opportunities.

I live in a way that works now. It more often allows me to feel in control of my destiny and my day-to-day functioning— even when things don't go as I would prefer. I more often trust my human self to make sound decisions because I trust my soul to always be there for me. I don't have to prove I am worthy before I can have that support. It's a 24/7 relationship that gives me the freedom to create, experiment, and follow inspirations, knowing that I am the best judge of how things turn out. Whether I am pleased or displeased, I get to choose what I will do with that result. I can find opportunities, decide how I will respond, or come to terms with the way a certain reality is for now. If others are judging me, I know they simply do not understand the nature of my journey.

These are the things that matter to me now. Of course, I am happy to welcome increased wellness in any measure that might unfold for me. I'm just relieved to know that I can experience joy and serenity without having to be perfect by some world standard. I am freed from the notion that I must change the way my body and mind operate to be an acceptable and accepted human being. Freedom is sweet.

Bibliography and Selected Resources

There are many helpful books and other products available now that deal with fibromyalgia, chronic fatigue syndrome, multiple chemical sensitivity, and spiritual and personal growth. Below are just a few that have been especially supportive of my own journey. Also listed are publications and productions referenced in the narrative.

Books

Adams, A. *Chronic Fatigue, ME, and Fibromyalgia: The Natural Recovery Plan.* London: Watkins Publishing, 2010.

Aron, E. N. *The Highly Sensitive Person.* New York: Broadway Books, 1996.

Bernhard, T. *How to be Sick: A Buddhist-Inspired Guide for the Chronically Ill and Their Caregivers.* Boston: Wisdom Publications, 2010.

Cooper, C. and J. Miller. *Integrative Therapies for Fibromyalgia, Chronic Fatigue Syndrome, and Myofascial Pain.* Rochester, VT: Healing Arts Press, 2010.

Donoghue, P. J. and M. E. Siegel. *Sick and Tired of Feeling Sick and Tired: Living With Invisible Chronic Illness.* New York: W. W. Norton & Company, Inc., 1992.

Ford, D. *The Dark Side of the Light Chasers.* New York: Riverhead Books, 1998.

Gibson, P. *Multiple Chemical Sensitivity.* Churchville, VA: Earthrive Books, 2006.

Gilbère, G. *I Was Poisoned by My Body.* Lancaster, OH: Lucky Press, 2001.

Lipscomb, A. *Poisoned by Pollution: An Unexpected Spiritual Journey.* Bloomington, IN: AuthorHouse, 2009.

Myss, C. *Sacred Contracts: Awakening Your Divine Potential.* New York: Three Rivers Press, 2002, 2003.

Orsborn, C. *Solved by Sunset.* New York: Harmony Books, 1995.

Ortner, N. *The Tapping Solution.* Carlsbad, CA: Hay House, Inc., 2013.

Rogers, S. A. *Wellness Against All Odds.* Syracuse, NY: Prestige Publishing, 1994.

Rose, E. *Lady of Gray Healing Candida: The Nightmare Chemical Epidemic.* Santa Monica, CA: Butterfly Publishing Company, 1985.

Scheinfeld, R. *The Invisible Path to Success.* Charlottesville, VA: Hampton Roads Publishing Company, Inc., 1998.

Starlanyl, D. and M. E. Copeland. *Fibromyalgia & Chronic Myofascial Pain.* Oakland, CA: New Harbinger Publications, Inc., 2001.

Audio Recording

Naparstek, B. *A Meditation to Help with Fibromyalgia & Chronic Fatigue* (Health Journeys Guided Imagery CD). Akron, OH: Image Paths, Inc., 2001.

Movies and Television

Homeland (TV Series) © 2012 Twentieth Century Fox Film Corporation.

Indiana Jones and The Last Crusade ™ and © 1989 by Lucasfilm Ltd. and Paramount Pictures.

It's a Wonderful Life © 1947 by Paramount Pictures.

Sleepless in Seattle © 1993 TriStar Pictures, Inc.

Star Trek: The Next Generation (TV Series) ™ and © 1992 by Paramount Pictures.

The Truman Show ™ and Copyright © 1998 Paramount Pictures.

The Wizard of Oz © 1939 by Warner Brothers.

Music

Noll, S. Singing Heart Productions. www.shainanoll.com.

Songs for the Inner Child, 1992.

Bread for the Journey, 1995.

You Can Relax Now, 2002.

Gupta, A. *The Advanced CFS/ME Recovery Programme with Ashok Gupta* (book and DVD). Swindon, UK: Gupta Amygdala Retraining, Harley Street Solutions LTD. www.guptaprogramme.com, 2008.

Notes

1   Quote permission granted at www.alancohen.com/contact/frequently-asked-questions.

2   Material excerpted from the book *Life is a Verb: 37 Days to Wake Up, Be Mindful, and Live Intentionally* ©2008 by Patricia Digh. Used with permission of Patricia Digh. (Guilford, CT, Skirt!, The Globe Pequot Press).

3   See *IL History and Philosophy: An Orientation for IL Staff* on-demand video modules at www.ilru.org/il-history-and-philosophy-orientation-for-il-staff.

4   A directory of all the centers for independent living in the US and territories is available at www.ilru.org.

5   DeJong, G. (October, 1979). Independent living: From social movement to analytic paradigm. *Archives of Physical Medicine and Rehabilitation*, vol. 60.

6   Retrieved from www.census.gov/newsroom/releases/archives/miscellaneous/cb12-134.html.

7   Retrieved from www.cdc.gov/chronicdisease/overview.

8   Retrieved from www.fmcpaware.org/aboutfibromyalgia.html.

9   Retrieved from www.cdc.gov/cfs/diagnosis.

10 Retrieved from www.ncbi.nlm.nih.gov/pmc/articles/PMC1448331.

11 Retrieved from www.chemicalsensitivityfoundation.org/mcs-prevalence.html.

12 Material excerpted from the book *The Invisible Path to Success* ©1998 by Robert Scheinfeld, used with permission from Hampton Roads Publishing c/o Red Wheel/Weiser, LLC Newburyport, MA and San Francisco, CA www.redwheelweiser.com.

[13] Retrieved from www.merriam-webster.com.

[14] Material excerpted from the book *So I'm God ... Now What?: Tools for Empowered Humans* by Steve Rother and the group ©2007 by Steve Rother. (Las Vegas, NV: Lightworker Publications), 80. www. Lightworker.com.

[15] Material excerpted from the book *Still Here: Embracing Aging, Changing, and Dying* © 2000 by Ram Dass, eds. Mark Matousek and Marlene Roeder, used with permission from Penguin Publishing Group, Penguin Random House, LLC, New York, NY.

[16] Quoted from *Star Trek: Into Darkness* ™ and ©2013 Paramount Pictures.

[17] See http://mn.gov/mnddc/parallels2/four/video/video44-tryanotherway.html.

[18] "How Could Anyone," words and music by Libby Roderick © Libby Roderick Music 1990 BMI. Used by permission. All rights reserved. From the recordings, *How Could Anyone* and *If You See a Dream*. Turtle Island Records: Anchorage, Alaska www.libbyroderick.com libbyroderick@gmail.com 907/278-6817.

[19] See www.TheTappingSolution.com.

[20] Material excerpted from the book *Poisoned by Pollution: An Unexpected Spiritual Journey* ©2009 by Anne Lipscomb, 174. Used by permission of Anne Lipscomb. www.annelipscomb.com.

[21] Material excerpted from the book *How to be Sick: A Buddhist-Inspired Guide for the Chronically Ill and Their Caregivers* ©2010 by Toni Bernhard. (Boston: Wisdom Publications, 2010, 118. Used by permission of Toni Bernhard. www.tonibernhard.com.

[22] Quoted with permission of Amina Donna Kruck. www.abil.org.

[23] Retrieved from www.merrian-webster.com.

[24] Quoted with permission of Ava Brenner. www.TheTransition.com.

Made in the USA
Middletown, DE
03 October 2020